domain.456

Problems in Society
Making Choices
Friendship

Linda Kondracki and Bev Gundersen

Cook Ministry Resources
a division of Cook Communications Ministries
Colorado Springs, Colorado/Paris, Ontario

domain.456: Problems in Society, Making Choices, Friendship

Scripture quotations are from the Holy Bible: New International Version (NIV), © 1973, 1978, 1984 by the International Bible Society. Used by permission of Zondervan Bible Publishers.

Published by Cook Ministry Resources
4050 Lee Vance View
Colorado Springs, CO 80918-7100
www. cookministries.com

Designed by Jeff Jansen
Illustrated by Sonny Carder
Printed in U.S.A.

ISBN: 0-7814-5517-0

Table of Contents ✓

Welcome to the Junior Electives Series

 Let's talk about it . . .

What is it like to grow up in America today? How do our junior-age children perceive the world around them, and their place in it? Did you know that your junior students are more aware of the world around them than any previous generation of American children? However, seen through their eyes the world is often seen as a scary and anxious place. Every day they are blatantly confronted with the threat of nuclear disasters, ecological concerns that warn them their planet may not exist by the time they grow up, and an increasing number of their classmates either wielding knives and guns at school or killed in gang-related incidents. Closer to home, you can expect a high number of your students to have experienced at least one divorce in their family, or suffered some kind of physical, sexual, or emotional abuse from family members.

As adults, we may like to close our eyes and see the days of childhood as carefree and innocent as they might have been in our day. But when we open our eyes and see the world as our kids see it today, it is clear that life holds much stress and anxiety for our children. Instead of wishing for simpler days, it is time for us to say to our kids, "Let's talk about it . . ."

The Junior Electives Series was designed to help you do just that. Each topic in the series was selected because it represents issues Juniors are concerned about, and in many cases learning about from their peers, the media, or in school. With the help of this curriculum, you will be able to provide an opportunity for them to discuss their concerns in a Christian context. For many of your kids, this may be the first chance they will have to hear that the Bible has a lot to teach them about each of these contemporary life concerns.

As you teach the lessons in this series, you will have an opportunity to:

• Introduce and teach topics of concern to Juniors in a distinctively Christian context.

• Provide a safe place to learn about, talk about, and express feelings about each issue.

• Teach practical skills and biblical principles Juniors can use to cope with each concern in their daily lives.

• Provide a tool to help parents facilitate family discussion and coping in the home setting.

 **Features of the Junior Elective Series**

Four-Part Lesson Plan

Each lesson follows this format:

1. Setting the Stage (5-10 minutes). Each lesson begins with an activity designed to do two things. First, it is a gathering activity, meaning that you can involve your students in it as soon as they arrive. You do *not* need to have the whole class present to begin your lesson time. By arriving early and having the Setting the Stage activity set up and ready for the kids as soon as they walk in the door, you will communicate a sense of excitement about the lesson and set a tone of orderliness for your class.

Secondly, the Setting the Stage activity is purposeful in that it will draw the students into the subject for the day. It is more than just something to keep the kids busy while everyone arrives. The activity will provide a fun and interesting way to draw the kids' attention to an area of interest in their lives. Most of the time, it will also raise questions which will lead them into the next section of the lesson.

2. Introducing the Issue (20 minutes). Building on the Setting the Stage activity, this section of the lesson will involve the kids in an active discussion of the topic of the day. The material provided for you contains information the kids need to know, anticipating key questions they may have. It also includes one or more learning activities particularly designed to encourage your students to talk about the issues most on their minds, while in the context of a Christian community. To make this time as effective as possible, you will need to establish your class as a safe place where everyone's feelings and questions are welcomed and treated seriously (some suggestions for doing that are listed on page 5). Once that has been accomplished, you may be surprised at how much your Juniors have to say, and the depth of their thinking!

3. Searching the Scriptures (20 minutes). This section of each lesson takes your class to the Bible to discover what God has to say about the topic being discussed. Your students may be amazed to find out just how much the Bible says about subjects that seem so *modern*. Through a wide variety of creative teaching methods, your class will study people and principles of Scripture that speak directly to the concerns gripping their hearts and minds. As you study together, you will also be acquainting them with the most valuable resource they can have for coping with these contemporary issues: their Bibles.

4. Living the Lesson (5-10 minutes). The final section of each lesson challenges the kids to take what they've learned and apply it to their own lives. It's the *so what* section. The class members will be encouraged to ask themselves, "So what am I going to do with what I've just learned?"

Clearly Stated Key Principles

Each book in the Junior Electives Series contains three units, each of which addresses a different topic of concern. The following three unit features will help your student focus on and remember the central principles of each unit.

1. Unit Verse. One verse has been chosen for each unit that summarizes the biblical principle central to the unit topic. The meaning of this verse is developed a little more each week as students work on a cooperative learning activity designed to help them understand and apply a key biblical principle.

2. Unit Affirmation. The primary learning objective for each unit has been phrased into an affirmation sentence that begins with "I can . . . " Discussing this affirmation each week will empower your students by letting them know they can do something positive about issues that may feel frightening or overwhelming.

3. Unit Service Projects. At the end of each unit you will find several ideas for your class to not only learn about the unit issue, but actually DO something about it. Although they are optional, taking the extra time to involve your class in a unit project will help them practice new skills and see for themselves that they can take an active role in the issues that affect their lives.

Parent Informational Letter

At the beginning of each unit, you will find PARTNERS . . . , a newsletter which you can photocopy and send home to the parents of your class members. This letter gives parents an overview of the topic being studied, as well as some practical ideas of ways they can further their child's learning through several Do-At-Home activities.

Flexibility and Variety

The Junior Electives Series has been designed to be usable in any number of settings. It is equally effective in a Sunday school setting, a Wednesday night series, or even a special setting such as a weekend retreat. If you live in an area that participates in release time, this series is an exellent resource to present biblical principles in a contemporary way. Feel free to be creative and find the best place for your group to talk about these important life principles.

A variety of learning activities are used to present the issue information and biblical truths. The following materials are considered standard supplies and are recommended to be available for the classtimes:

- Bibles
- Glue
- Tape
- Pencils
- Scissiors
- Stapler
- Paper

 **A Word About Children and Stress . . .**

As you prepare to teach the Junior Electives Series, it is important to realize that many of the subjects you will be studying are the sources of stress in the lives of your students. Many students may never have had the chance to talk openly about these issues, and doing so in your class may well raise their anxiety level. Throughout these sessions, there are several things you can keep in mind:

1) Point them to Jesus. Perhaps the greatest benefit of the Junior Elective Series is that it will give you the opportunity to help your kids learn that a relationship to Jesus Christ is the best resource we can have to face the stressful, anxious parts of our lives. Through the Bible studies and your own personal witness of the power of Christ in your life, you can have the privilege of introducing children to Jesus and inviting them to ask Him to be an active part of their lives.

2) Create a safe place where they can talk about their real feelings. Children have a strong tendency to say the things in class that they think teachers want to hear. Early on in this series, you will want to create a safe place for sharing by continually reassuring your kids that they can say what is really on their minds, and making a rule that no one can criticize or make fun of anything anyone else shares in class. In many cases, expressing their feelings in a safe place, and having those feelings accepted by you and the class will relieve much of their anxiety.

3) If necessary, help them get outside help. You may find a child in your class who is experienceing an unusual amount of stress. In that case, ask your pastor or Christian Education Director for the procedure your church uses to refer children and families for professional help.

In the Know...

Children today are more aware of the large-scale problems in our world than any previous generation. So much so that anxiety over societal problems is a significant source of stress for your junior-age kids. Unlike times past, however, little attempt is being made to protect your kids from dealing with these problems. In fact, the reverse is true and children are being educated about them at younger and younger ages.

In this unit, you and your Juniors will explore four problems high on the list of concerns for this age group. As you do, you will want to be sensitive to the stress your kids may be feeling about each of these subjects, and keep in mind that much of their stress comes from feeling small and powerless in the face of such large and extensive problems. However, this unit will give you an opportunity to reduce that stress by assuring them that God is still in control and that He invites us to be partners with Him in caring about these issues; you can give them courage to be the lighthouse of God's love on their world.

Through the use of the Unit Verse and the Unit Affirmation, you will help them understand that big problems are managed as each of us does small acts of kindness in Jesus' name.

✔ Problems in Society Overview

Unit Verse: Command them to do good, to be rich in good deeds, and to be generous and willing to share. I Timothy 6:18

Unit Affirmation: I CAN MAKE A DIFFERENCE!

LESSON	TITLE	OBJECTIVE	SCRIPTURE BASE
Lesson #1	Give Us This Day Our Daily Bread (and Bed)	That your students will help the homeless and hungry because this is the same as helping Jesus.	Matthew 25:31-40
Lesson #2	Rich Man, Poor Man, Beggar man, Thief	That your students will be able to recognize dangers of materialism and follow God's urging to share their possessions with people in need.	Matthew 19:16-23
Lesson #3	How Do You Spell Heartache? A-I-D-S	That your students will understand what AIDS is and follow Jesus' example by showing compassion for those suffering fromm it.	Mark 1:40-42
Lesson #4	Ganging Up 'n You	That your students will turn to God and Christian peer groups instead of violent gangs to satisfy their need of belonging.	Proverbs 1:10-19

Partners

Keeping Parents Informed and Involved!

For the next few weeks your junior-age child will be part of a group learning about Problems in Society. *Partners* is a planned parent piece to keep you informed of what will be taught during this exciting series.

PREVIEW...
Problems in Society

In the past few decades, the world has become an unfriendly and scary place to many children. At one time, subjects such as homelessness, hunger, AIDS, and crimes of violence were far from the minds of junior-age kids. Today, however, your children are constantly hearing about a whole range of serious, large-scale problems.

If your kids are like most kids today, they are worrying a lot about the problems they see around them. And, being "just kids," they are no doubt feeling small and powerless in the shadow of problems of such magnitude. After all, what can one "little kid" do about an epidemic of AIDS, or the large number of kids bringing knives and guns to school?

As parents and teachers, now is the time for us to help our children develop healthy attitudes toward the problems they see in their communities and world. We can empower them to face the future with a sense of purpose and challenge, instead of fear or hopelessness. By assuring them that God is still in control, and that He gives each of us the privilege of being partners with Him in caring about the world's problems, we can give kids courage to get involved in social issues, rather than "checking out."

In the weeks ahead, your kids will learn that big problems are best handled as each of us does a small part. As they review the Unit Verse and Unit Affirmation each week, they will see that small acts of kindness done in Jesus' name make all the difference in the world!

Unit Verse:
Command them to do good, to be rich in good deeds, and to be generous and willing to share. I Timothy 6:18

Unit Affirmation:
I CAN MAKE A DIFFERENCE!

PRINCIPLES...
Problems in Society

This unit on societal problems will focus on four problems high on the list of concerns for Juniors. They are:

THE HUNGRY AND THE HOMELESS.

Thousands of individuals and families are homeless and hungry in America today. Through looking at Jesus' words in Matthew 25:31-40, your kids will see that God calls each of us to care about others who are without life's most basic needs.

POVERTY AND MATERIALISM.

A close look at advertising will help your kids evaluate *why* they buy the things they do. They will also look at the myth that says how many *things* they have is the measure of how successful they are in life. As they study Matthew 19:16-23, they will hear Jesus' words telling them that their relationship to God is the most important part of life, and the more we use our *things* to care for others, the more successful we are in His eyes.

AIDS.

Fear of AIDS and people who have AIDS is one of the greatest concerns on the minds of kids today. In addition to receiving accurate information about AIDS, your Juniors will be helped by observing and following Jesus' example in Mark 1:40-42. Getting over our fears will allow us to see the suffering of people (including kids) who have AIDS and reach out to them with Jesus' love.

GANGS, CRIME AND VIOLENCE.

More and more young children in every community are turning to gangs as a way to find belonging and acceptance in a society that feels scary and threatening. Your kids will talk about why gang membership may look good at first, but can only hurt them in the end. They will also see that gang membership is not new, and read what God's Word has to say about it in Proverbs 1:10-19.

PRACTICE...
Making a Difference in Societal Problems

You can take an active role in helping your kids face the problems around them, and reach out in Jesus' name. Here are a few ideas to get you started:

1. NAMING OUR FEARS.

The first step to overcoming our

fears is to name them. Ask your children to make a list of five or six things they and other kids their age fear the most. Talk about each fear on their list, keeping in mind the following questions:

• Do they need more information? Accurate information is important to taking away the fear and developing a healthy attitude. Visit your local library, or call your child's school and ask for the information you need.

• Is there something you can do about the problem? Getting involved is always less fearful than sitting around worrying about it! Writing a letter, visiting someone, reaching out to others in need, etc., are important activities for your kids to learn.

• Are there safety lessons to be taught? Does your child know what to do if a classmate brings a gun or knife to school? Be aware of the safety issues connected with each of the fears on the list.

2. SUPPORT LOCAL FOOD PANTRIES AND CLOTHING CLOSETS.

Teach your children to share

what they have by bringing items on a regular basis. Let them clean out their closets and pack up their outgrown clothes and no longer needed toys. Take them shopping to buy food items. When you deliver the items, ask the people in charge to explain how the pantry or closet works. If possible, come every so often and volunteer your time, as well. Developing a sensitivity to the less fortunate is an important part of our Christian lives.

3. GANG PREVENTION.

The greatest reason kids give for joining violent gangs is no sense of belonging at home. Prevent the need for your child to turn to a gang by strengthening your family times. Talking with your kids and planning family outings NOW will help them find love and acceptance from you and not on the streets.

4. PRIME-TIME PRAYER TIME.

As a family, pray specifically about the issues of homelessness and hunger, materialism, AIDS, and gangs. You might include prayer for those in leadership of organizations designed to help the homeless, the families and friends of those with AIDS as well as victims themselves, the needs of the kids who are joining up with gangs, and wisdom to make decisions regarding the purchases that your family may be making in the near future.

Lesson 1 ✔

Give Us This Day Our Daily Bread (and Bed)

Aim: That your students will help the homeless and hungry because this is the same as helping Jesus.

Scripture: Matthew 25:31-40

Unit Verse: Command them to do good, to be rich in good deeds, and to be generous and willing to share. I Timothy 6:18

Unit Affirmation: I CAN MAKE A DIFFERENCE!

 **Planning Ahead**

1. Prepare the Unit Affirmation poster by writing the following on a large poster board: I CAN MAKE A DIFFERENCE! Under the title write the numbers 1-4 vertically along the left-hand side.
2. Prepare snacks and slips of paper as described in INTRODUCING THE ISSUE.
3. Photocopy activity sheets (pages 15 and 16)—one for each student.

1 Setting the Stage (5-10 minutes)

WHAT YOU'LL DO
- Prepare a bulletin board or mural to use for the Unit Verse each week during this unit

WHAT YOU'LL NEED
- newsprint or an attractive paper for the background and border strips
- yarn
- magazines and newspapers that contain pictures of or words describing the homeless and hungry

2 Introducing the Issue (20 minutes)

WHAT YOU'LL DO
- Participate in an activity to introduce the concept that life isn't always fair
- Use an activity sheet to discuss reasons why people are homeless and hungry, and the problems they face
- Introduce the Unit Affirmation Poster

WHAT YOU'LL NEED
- Snacks
- Slips of colored paper
- "What's Wrong Here?" Activity Sheet (page 15)
- Unit Affirmation Poster

3 Searching the Scriptures (20 minutes)

WHAT YOU'LL DO
- Read the Scripture passage and discuss ways Juniors can meet the needs of the hungry and homeless
- Present an object lesson to demonstrate how helping the needy is really serving Jesus

WHAT YOU'LL NEED
- Bibles
- Real or play money

4 Living the Lesson (5-10 minutes)

WHAT YOU'LL DO
- Show ways Juniors can help the hungry and homeless by cutting out pictures and gluing them onto an activity sheet

WHAT YOU'LL NEED
- "Thanks, I Needed That" Activity Sheet (page 16)
- Old magazines and newspapers

✓ Setting the Stage (5-10 minutes)

As your students arrive, involve them in some aspect of setting up a bulletin board or mural that the class will be using with the Unit Verse during this unit on Problems in Society.

If a bulletin board is available, allow some kids to pin or staple the background paper in place, others can measure and cut strips for the border, and someone else can use the yarn to divide the board into four sections. If you are making a mural, use a large piece of newsprint. Have the students draw or attach a border and divide the mural into the four sections. Ask students who are artistic or good printers to prepare the captions. You will need the Unit Verse printed out to be used as a title for the board, and two smaller captions for today's section, "Hungry" and "Homeless."

As students complete their assignments, ask them to look through the magazines and newspapers and cut out pictures of or words that describe people helping the hungry and homeless. Guide the conversation to focus on the Juniors' encounter with the hungry and homeless. **Have you ever seen a homeless person? What do you think about when you see someone who doesn't have a home? How does what you see make you feel?** Set these pictures aside for use in SEARCHING THE SCRIPTURES. **For the next four weeks, we will be talking about some problems facing our society. These are not new problems, but ones that are important for us as Christians to understand and care about. Before we get started though, I brought us a small snack to share.**

✓ Introducing the Issue (20 minutes)

As a way to teach your kids that not everyone has the same advantages in life, handle the snack time in the following manner. Bring cupcakes or brownies for about half your class; apple slices or raisins for another 40% of the class; and white crackers for the remaining 10%. Then, prepare slips of colored paper

to determine who will get what snack (50% red slips, 40% blue, and 10% green).

As you prepare for the snack, pass out the slips of paper to the class. Then, instruct the students that all those with green slips are to sit on the floor at the back of the room. Everyone else can sit with you around the table(s). Distribute the snacks to the kids according to the color of paper they are holding. Bring the crackers to the greens last. While they are eating, carefully observe the dynamics of the group. When they are done, invite the green group to join you at the table again. **What do you think about our snack time today?** Give kids an opportunity to tell their reactions. Those with the crackers will probably have a lot to say. **How did our class handle this situation: Did anyone complain? Did anyone do anything to try to get a better snack? Did anyone reach out and share what they had with others who had less? How did it feel to be in the green group? How did it feel to be in the red group?**

Summarize the discussion by emphasizing that the way snack time was handled wasn't really fair. Explain that many things in life are not always fair. **Many people within our country today do not have homes or jobs and that makes life very painful. At the same time, many others live in huge homes in very beautiful neighborhoods. For those who are living on the street or in shelters, that doesn't feel any more fair than my giving some of you crackers for snack today. Let's take a closer look at the problem of the homeless and hungry, and what it means for us as Christians.** Distribute copies of the activity sheet, "What's Wrong Here?" page 15. Read the first statement together and allow the students to give their responses. **The answer is** *false*. **Although we are one of the richest nations in the world, many families in our nation go to bed hungry at night because there is no money to buy food.**

Continue through the next four statements. The answer to the second statement is *false*. **Most people who are homeless are there because of circumstances beyond their control. Life isn't always fair, and some people experience things that make them homeless.** Examples of such experiences are: loss of a job and can't find another one that pays the same amount of money; a serious illness takes all the money a family had saved plus they have to sell their house to pay all the bills; a natural disaster destroys a house and the family cannot afford to start over. In addition, thousands within our country can't read or write and have no skills to get a job that will pay them a good wage.

The answer to the third statement is *false*. **Having a job doesn't always pay the bills. It is very expensive to provide for a family these days, and**

many people simply don't have the right kind of skills to get jobs that pay enough. So, they cannot afford a house and food for their families. The answer to the fourth statement is *false*. Explain that about one third of all homeless people are children. Whole families can become homeless for unexpected reasons. Sometimes the only answer is for the family to split up and the children are put into foster homes.

Finally, the answer to the last statement is *false*. **You are never too young to care about problems in our society. You may not be able to solve the causes of the problem, but there are many small things you can do to make a difference in other people's lives. We'll talk more about what we can do a little later today.**

Display the Unit Affirmation poster where everyone can see it and you can easily write on it. Ask the class to read it aloud together. **The world is not always a happy place. For many, it is a difficult and sad place to live. Jesus asks us to care about people who struggle through life, and to share with them what we can. You may think you are just a kid, but always remember, YOU CAN MAKE A DIFFERENCE!** Remind the kids that one way they can make a difference is by caring for the homeless and hungry. After the number one, write, *by caring for the homeless and hungry.*

Now let's find out how we can do this by taking a closer look at God's Word.

Searching the Scriptures (20 minutes)

The problems of hunger and homelessness are not new. In Bible times there were many people who had no place to live and who often had to beg for food. Religious Jews often gave to these people because they thought these acts would help them earn their way to heaven. Jesus wanted people to understand it is impossible for them to pay for their sins and be good enough to get into heaven. He explained to His followers the real reason for helping the homeless and hungry. Have your students turn to Matthew 25:34-40 in their Bibles. Read this passage together. Kids can take turns reading verses while the rest of the class follows along in their Bibles.

Who is the King in this parable? (Jesus.) **What do you suppose the people Jesus was talking to thought when they heard what He said?** The students' answers will be speculation, however, they may believe that the people realized the importance of helping others or the people may have been confused about how helping others was the same as helping the King.

Even though Jesus told that parable long ago, the importance of helping others is something that we need to keep in mind today. Bring the idea of the importance of helping others home to your students' lives by talking about each need and how they can get personally involved in meeting them. **How can you feed the hungry?** (Collect and donate food and money to food shelves; have projects such as selling recycled pop cans, walks for hunger, or car washes where the proceeds are used for the hungry; go without snacks and save the money to give to the hungry; grow a garden so you can share the vegetables.)

Usually when we think of caring for the sick we think of being a doctor or nurse, or visiting patients in a hospital. Can you think of other ways to look after people who are sick? (When patients are home you can send cards, bring gifts, go visit, or call them on the phone; bring and help explain school assignments to homebound classmates; help out with meals and other chores when parents are caring for sick people.)

How can you invite a stranger in? (Become a friend with a new kid in your school or neighborhood; have new people from church over for a meal; help people at a homeless shelter by visiting them, playing games with children there, or contributing blankets.) **What are some ways you can give clothing?** (Collect and recycle outgrown, no-longer-used items; give money to buy new things.)

Discuss how "prison" can mean more than a jail cell. It might be a nursing home where the elderly feel confined. Even a difficult situation such as an abusive family problem or a drug addiction is a type of prison. Homeless people may feel as limited as if they were in jail. **How can you visit needy people in these kinds of prisons?** (Go to see them; call on the phone; send cards; write letters; bring them home to visit with your family; pray for them.)

Present the following object lesson in order to illustrate what Jesus meant when He said that by helping the needy we are helping Him. Call two of your students to you. **Let's play a little game of *Suppose*. Let's suppose** (name of kid A) **is hungry and needs food.** Have this student stand aside while you continue the object lesson with the other kid. **Let's also suppose that** (name of kid B) **is a very good friend of mine. I meet him/her one day and say, "How would you like to go with me to McDonald's restaurant for burgers and soft drinks?" Now suppose when we get there** (kid B) **has no money for food, so I loan him/her some money to buy it.** (Give real or play money to student.) Say with humor, **Of course** (kid B) **is very grateful, thanks me, buys a burger and soda, and says, "I'll pay you back."** Pause for kid to say this. If s/he doesn't you can give a humorous hint to do so.

Suppose I tell (kid B) **s/he can pay me back by giving the money to** (kid A) **instead of to me because I know that** (kid A) **really needs it and I want him/her to have it.** Conclude this illustration by having (kid B) give (kid A) the money and both students return to their places.

Explain to your students that that is a picture of what Jesus has done. He is the one who gives us everything we have: food; clothing; home; friends; people to take care of us. We want to show Him our thanks and how much we love Him. He tells us we can pay Him back by giving those same things to people who really need them. Point out to your students that the kind of help Jesus wants them to give involves more than just material things. All needy people have one thing in common. They are people. That means they have feelings just like you. They smile and laugh when they are happy, cry when they are sad, are proud of doing something well. Helping the homeless and hungry means extending friendship and love to them as well as money or material items.

Review the ways you previously discussed regarding how to help the hungry and homeless. Point out that by doing these things your kids are also showing their love to Jesus. **When we love Jesus we do things for Him gladly and willingly. This attitude brings great joy to ourselves, God, and those they help.**

Have your students choose two pictures or phrases from those that were cut out during SETTING THE STAGE to display with the "Hungry" and "Homeless" captions. Add these visuals and captions to the bulletin board or mural.

 Living the Lesson (5-10 minutes)

We've talked in general terms about how you can show your love for Jesus and help meet the needs of these people. Now you are going to have the opportunity to show how you would help some specific people. Hand out the *Thanks, I Needed That,* activity sheet (page 16), depicting some problems of the hungry and homeless. Working in pairs, have your students look through old magazines and newspapers and cut out pictures or words representing ways they can meet each need. They will then glue these to the sheet by each problem. If they are unable to find what they need in the magazines and newspapers or the kids enjoy art, they could draw the pictures instead.

Close class with a prayer similar to this one. **Dear Jesus, we want to thank You for all the things You have given us and show our love for You by helping others. Help us take advantage of opportunities to help the hungry and homeless. In Your name we pray. Amen.**

What's Wrong Here?

Look at each of the statements below and decide if it is mostly True, or mostly False. If you think it is false, write a new sentence below it that is true.

1. In our country, people don't go to bed hungry at night because their family can't afford to buy food. **True?? False??**

Rewrite:_____
_____
_____

2. People who are homeless are that way because they want to be or because they are too lazy to get a job. **True?? False??**

Rewrite:_____
_____
_____

3. Having a job always means you will have enough money to pay rent and buy food. **True?? False??**

Rewrite:_____
_____
_____

4. Only weird adults are homeless. **True?? False??**

Rewrite:_____
_____
_____
_____

5. There is nothing I can do about the homeless and hungry. I'm too young to make a difference in such a large problem. **True?? False??**

Rewrite:_____
_____
_____
_____

 # Thanks, I Needed That!

Glue or draw pictures in the spaces to show how you can serve Jesus by helping these needy people.

Juan Ortiz and his family left home to work as field workers in a northern state for the summer. When they got there the crops were poor because of lack of rain so nobody was hiring extra help. Now Juan and his family are stranded in a strange place with no money to get home, no place to stay, and not enough to eat.

Caleb Jackson is in your class. His dad lost his job when the company he worked for went bankrupt. The family had to give up their house and car and move into a tiny apartment downtown. You notice that Caleb sometimes doesn't bring a lunch to school or have money to buy his lunch. He often asks for food from others.

Rich Man, Poor Man, Beggar Man, Thief

Aim: That your students will be able to recognize the dangers of materialism and follow God's urging to share their possessions with people in need.

Scripture: Matthew 19:16-23

Unit Verse: Command them to do good, to be rich in good deeds, and to be generous and willing to share. I Timothy 6:18

Unit Affirmation: I CAN MAKE A DIFFERENCE!

 **Planning Ahead**

1. Make caption, "Poverty and Materialism," to add to the Unit Bulletin Board or Mural.
2. Cut out a few pictures from magazines or newspapers of people sharing what they have with others.
3. Optional–Videotape of TV ads
4. Photocopy activity sheets (pages 23 and 24)–one for each student.

1 Setting the Stage (5-10 minutes)

WHAT YOU'LL DO

- Make an advertisement collage

WHAT YOU'LL NEED

- Magazines and other materials that have a lot of advertisements in them

2 Introducing the Issue (20 minutes)

WHAT YOU'LL DO

- Define "success" from the viewpoint of advertising
- Use an activity sheet to discover how much materialism is a part of their personal value system
- Add a phrase to the Unit Affirmation Poster

WHAT YOU'LL NEED

- "It's Important to Me . . ."Activity Sheet (page 23)
- Unit Affirmation Poster
- OPTIONAL: A TV and VCR, and a tape of TV ads

3 Searching the Scriptures (20 minutes)

WHAT YOU'LL DO

- Dramatize a story that shows what God's word says about attitudes toward riches
- Use a group object lesson to demonstrate the temporary enjoyment of materialistic things

WHAT YOU'LL NEED

- Bibles
- "Life-Styles of the Rich and . . . Sad" Activity Sheet (page 24)
- Small piece of fast-melting candy for each student

4 Living the Lesson (5-10 minutes)

WHAT YOU'LL DO

- Make an inventory of possessions to discover what can be shared to help other people

WHAT YOU'LL NEED

- Paper and pencils

☑ Setting the Stage (5-10 minutes)

Bring to class a stack of old magazines, newspapers, junk mail, and anything else that contains a lot of advertisements and spread these out on the table. As your students arrive, involve them in making an advertisement collage by cutting out ads and gluing them onto 12" x 18" paper. (If you prefer, you could use a strip of shelf paper and let students work together on one large collage.) Instruct the kids to completely fill their paper, overlapping the ads in a pleasing layout.

Talk with your students about the ads they are finding. **What is your favorite advertisement? Do you believe everything you see in the ads? Have you ever been influenced by an advertisement to go out and buy something? What was it?**

When the collages are finished, have your students use a black marker to write in large letters over the top of the ads, "WHAT'S THE MESSAGE?" Students can keep these close by, or they can tape them to the wall where you can refer to them a little later.

☑ Introducing the Issue (20 minutes)

Today we are going to talk about a very important subject. To get started let's take a look at this person. Draw a stick figure on the chalkboard or piece of poster board. **Let's think of some things that will show that this is a *successful* person. In order to do that, we have to make a list of the things that we think make a person successful. As you grow up, what are the things you think will make you successful?** Let kids respond. When they mention things that you can draw, add them to the picture. Other things you can write off to the side. Examples of things the kids might say are: live in a big house, have lots of friends, be a doctor or lawyer, drive a certain kind of car, be famous, etc. Encourage them to think of as many things as possible. **How many of the things we listed involve having a lot of money and expensive possessions?** Put a check mark by these items. **How important are material possessions to being a successful person? Can we be a success without a lot of things?** Let the kids respond. If they say "yes," encourage them to elaborate on what nonmaterial values, characteristics, or traits make a person successful.

What does our society tell us is the measure of success? Let your class respond. Summarize by telling them that often the people who are considered successful in our country are those who are wealthy. The wealthier a person is the more successful that person is viewed to be. **Where do we get that idea?**

OPTIONAL: If you have a VCR available to you, you might consider taping a series of TV commercials at home this week, and showing them to the class at this time.

Refer to the collages the kids made earlier, and the video if you used it. Point out to the class that advertising is a big source of messages we receive every day. One advertising company estimated that every American sees 10,000 advertising messages on TV, in magazines, and other places EVERY DAY! **What are all these messages telling us?** (We need these products; we won't be successful unless we have these products; our lives are incomplete without these products.) Guide your students to see that advertising not only tells us to buy things, it also tells us that we won't be happy or successful until we have the product! **Since we see so many ads every day, we are taught that** *things* **are what bring us happiness and success.**

What are the messages advertisers are giving to kids today about what you need to be happy and successful? (Have to have Nintendo, designer clothes, tape players and the "right" tapes, certain cereals and snacks, etc.) **Are the advertisers really that concerned with your happiness and success?** (No.) **Why do they give us these messages?** (So they can sell their products to us, making them successful!)

What does God say about what makes us successful people? Read Matthew 6:31-34 together and discover what Jesus said about the value of possessions. **Can a person have very few possessions and still be successful?** (Yes.) **What is really important in life?** Give your class some time to think about this question. It's okay to have a few seconds of silence.

Summarize by emphasizing that it is not wrong to have possessions. There are some things people need in order to live and function in their surroundings. What we must guard against is getting to the point where we have to have certain things, or we think that the greatest success in life is to have more and more *things*. The danger is that when *things* are that important to us, we start caring less about people and start thinking too much about how to get what we want.

Distribute copies of the activity sheet, "It's Important to Me . . ." (page 23) and scissors. **Sometimes we can get a better idea of what we really believe is important by doing an activity such as this one. Please be completely honest in doing this, and don't do it in a way that you think is** *right* **for Christians. There is no right or wrong way to do this.**

Following the directions on the sheet, give kids time to complete the project.

Then, talk about the choices they made and why. End this section by encouraging everyone, including yourself, to keep the really important things in life in perspective.

Refer to the Unit Affirmation poster from last week. Read the affirmation through again, and the phrase you added last week. Ask the kids to think of a phrase they could add this week. Example might be: "... by not being greedy," or "... by seeking God's kingdom first," or "... by sharing my possessions with others." When you have selected a phrase, add it to the poster. **Now let's see what Jesus said to one person about the importance of** *things* **in his life.**

Searching the Scriptures (20-25 minutes)

In Bible times, people believed that being rich was a sign that God was blessing you because you were a good person. Wealthy people often had an attitude that they were better than others. Jesus had some very strong things to say about people's attitudes towards possessions. Let's turn to Matthew 19:16-23 in our Bibles to see what He taught.

Hand out "Life-Styles of the Rich and . . . Sad," activity sheet (page 24). Today's Bible study is presented as a dramatization. You will need seven volunteers to read the parts of Anna; Enos; Jacob; Jesus; Person #1; Person #2; and Person #3. If your class is small you may choose to take a part yourself and/or have kids read more than one part. To add an extra touch of realism to the drama, you could use a large spoon or disconnected microphone for Enos to use and extend to people when he interviews them. If your students enjoy drama they can act this out.

After you have finished, hand out a small piece of quick-melting candy to each student. **You all did so well reading and following this story that I have something for you.** This candy will help you point out the fleeting nature of material possessions later on in the lesson.

What kind of a person was the young man who came to Jesus? (Good; religious; rich.) Point out that although he had been trying to obey and please God he realized that something was missing from his life and came to Jesus to find out what it was. **What did Jesus say he should do?** (Sell his things; give to the poor; follow Him.) **Why do you think he turned away from Jesus when he found out what he needed to do?** (He didn't want to give up everything; Jesus made it too hard to follow Him.)

What did the people in the drama say about Jesus' command? (Rich people deserved to be rich because they were good; poor people were poor because they were bad; if everybody gave up their possessions they would all be too poor to take care of themselves; Jesus was right because the man loved things more than he loved God.)

What did Jesus say about rich people entering the kingdom of heaven? (It is hard for them to do it.) **Why do you think He said this?** (They are tempted to make *things* a greater priority in their lives than God; they become selfish and forget God.) **Do you think all Christians should get rid of their money and possessions?** Your students will probably have mixed opinions. Emphasize that things themselves aren't the problem. Instead it is our attitude toward them. God has given us everything we have and we can be thankful to Him for them. But when our desire for things becomes greater than our love for God and people, something terrible happens. Instead of us owning the possessions, they own us. We become involved with protecting them, accumulating more, and fear losing them. Then, like this rich young man, we miss out on the greatest thing of all—close fellowship with God.

OPTIONAL: Sometimes students feel that because you are a teacher, you no longer have problems. To help your kids identify with you, share a struggle you have with materialism. Here are some tips on how to tell if your attitude toward things is in trouble: You insist on getting things no matter what the results are for others; you quickly lose interest in them after you get them; you spend less time enjoying them than letting others know you have them; you junk them only to rush out and get more.

Have the class read the Unit Verse together from I Timothy 6:18. "Command them to do good, to be rich in good deeds, and to be generous and willing to share." **How long did the candy I gave you last?** (Not very long.) **How did it taste?** (Good.) **Did any of you want more when it was gone?**

Imagine that the candy was your favorite belonging. Just like the candy, our possessions seem great while they last. The trouble is they don't last very long. Material riches quickly disappear. Things never fully satisfy you but only lead to a desire for more. A millionaire was asked, "How much money would it take to make you happy?" His answer was, "Just a little bit more." Although he was extremely wealthy he wasn't satisfied.

Point out that satisfaction comes not from gathering things but from giving things away. When we are generous and share our things to help others we become rich in good deeds. This kind of wealth brings joy and satisfaction to both the giver and receiver. It becomes our treasure in heaven which can't be stolen and will never rust or decay. It lasts forever.

Have your students help you choose a picture from the ones you have cut from magazines for the bulletin board or mural to go along with the heading,

"Poverty and Materialism." It should be one which illustrates sharing what they have to benefit others. Place the picture and caption the bulletin board or mural.

✓ Living the Lesson (5-10 minutes)

Most of us have more than we think we have. You are going to take an inventory to let you see how rich you really are. Pass out pieces of paper and pencils and have your students make as complete a list of their possessions as they can. Some items that can be included are: clothing; sports gear; entertainment items; jewelry; cosmetics; books; hobby supplies. They should also include the quantities of each item if possible.

After they have spent some time on this inventory show them how to find things they can share with others. **Look over your list. Circle items that you use very little, are duplicates, or you don't really need. A good test is to ask yourself, "How much is enough?" What are some ways you could share these possessions with people in need?** Brainstorm ways they can collect and recycle these items through church or social agencies. If your church doesn't already do this, perhaps you would like to start a sharing program.

Perhaps you have heard that "more is better" or "riches are an indication of God's blessings." Or perhaps you believe that people are in poverty because they are lazy or ignorant and don't try to take care of themselves and their families. None of these things are true. A variety of circumstances causes people to find themselves in need of money, clothing, and other material needs. Jesus says to share what we have with others. Sharing out of love helps eliminate poverty and draws people together. It brings riches that never pass away. Only really important things like love, trust, and knowing Jesus as Savior and Lord endure. These treasures can be shared with those in need and the results enjoyed forever.

Close with a song of thanksgiving for God's many gifts to us. "Thank You, Lord" is an excellent choice. You might also ask volunteers to pray asking God to help them share their possessions with others.

It's Important to Me... ✔

Cut the squares apart and lay them out in front of you. Then, arrange them in the order of their importance to you.

Wearing the "Right" Clothes

Having Many Friends

Spending Time with My Family

Making Lots of Money

Getting Good Grades

Having the Latest Music

Knowing God

Being Kind to Others

Being Good in Sports

Life-Styles of the Rich and...Sad

ANCHORWOMAN ANNA: This is Channel 6, KJER News. We interrupt our regular programming to bring you this special news bulletin. Enos ben Joseph has been following the exciting new teacher, Jesus, in His travels across the country. What's happening there, Enos?

ENOS: The crowd is really buzzing here, Anna. Jacob ben Silas, son of the wealthy and famous member of the Sanhedrin council, has just come to Jesus. This is quite an opportunity for Jesus to boost His image. Jacob appears to have a question for the teacher. Let's get closer and listen to their conversation.

JACOB: Teacher, what good thing must I do to get eternal life?

JESUS: Why do you ask Me about what is good? There is only One who is good. If you want to enter eternal life, obey the commandments.

JACOB: Which ones?

JESUS: Do not murder, do not commit adultery, do not steal, do not give false testimony, honor your father and mother, and love your neighbor as yourself.

JACOB: All these I have kept. What do I still lack?

JESUS: If you want to be perfect, go, sell your possessions and give to the poor, and you will have treasure in heaven. Then come, follow Me.

ENOS: This is amazing. Jacob is turning away and leaving. Jesus is making no effort to stop him. Doesn't He understand what a great help this wealthy young man could be to His career? Wait a minute, Jesus is talking to His followers.

JESUS: I tell you the truth; it is hard for a rich man to enter the kingdom of heaven.

ANNA: Enos, what does Jesus mean by that statement?

ENOS: I'm not sure. I'll talk to some of the people in the crowd to get their reaction to this turn of events. What do you make of this?

PERSON #1: It doesn't make any sense. Jacob already said he kept the commandments and we can see God has blessed him. Everyone knows that riches are God's reward for a good life. It's easy to tell what someone is like by just looking at what he has. If someone is poor then we know he is a bad person.

ENOS: Thank you for that comment. Here's another person who looks like s/he has a different opinion of things. What do you say?

PERSON #2: It's obvious that Jesus has been under too much stress. Why, it would be crazy for a person to sell all his possessions and give the money to the poor. Then who would take care of him now that he, too, is poor?

PERSON #3 (breaking in): I think you're both wrong. Jesus didn't mean those things at all.

ENOS: And what do you think He meant?

PERSON #3: Didn't you see the expression on Jacob's face when Jesus told him to sell his possessions? He looked like he had been told to give up his best friend.

ENOS: Which means what?

PERSON #3: Jacob hinted that obeying all the commandments proved he loved God. But I think Jesus put His finger right on the heart of the problem. Jacob loves his possessions more than anything else. He's allowed them to have first place in his life. Jesus wanted him to change his attitude about them.

ENOS: Then you think that more isn't always better?

PERSON #3: Not when it takes the place of God in your life. Then having things can be downright dangerous!

ENOS: Well, that is certainly a new thought and one that might mean a lot of changes for some people. That pretty well wraps up things here. This is Enos ben Joseph on the trail with Jesus and His disciples. Now back to the studio and you, Anna.

ANNA: Thank you for that report, Enos. And now back to our regular program.

Activity Sheet by Bev Gundersen © 1991 David C. Cook Publishing Co. Permission granted to reproduce for classroom use only.

How Do You Spell Heartache? A -I- D-S

Aim: That your students will understand what AIDS is and follow Jesus' example by showing compassion for those suffering from it.

Scripture: Mark 1:40-42

Unit Verse: Command them to do good, to be rich in good deeds, and to be generous and willing to share. I Timothy 6:18

Unit Affirmation: I CAN MAKE A DIFFERENCE!

 Planning Ahead

1. Letter the following phrases on strips of paper: Welcome to Friendly Feud!; Kidnapping (20 points); Nuclear War (30 points); and AIDS (50 points).
2. Make a caption, "AIDS," to add to the Unit Bulletin Board or Mural.
3. Cut out a few pictures showing people reaching out to help patients with AIDS or any similar illness.
4. Photocopy activity sheets (pages 31 and 32)–one for each student.
5. Make face paint for LIVING THE LESSON by mixing two teaspoons cornstarch and one teaspoon cold cream in a small container until well blended. Add one teaspoon water. Stir until smooth. Add blue and red food coloring one drop at a time until mixture is purple and not too thin. Store in a covered container. If you have a large class you may want to increase the amounts to make more paint.
6. Optional–Call your local school district and ask for information on AIDS education materials being used in your students' school(s). This will help you know what your students have already been told about AIDS.

1 Setting the Stage (5-10 minutes)

WHAT TO DO

- Play "Friendly Feud" as a way to discover three fears kids have

WHAT YOU'LL NEED

- Headings for "Friendly Feud"
- Paper and pencils

2 Introducing the Issue (20 minutes)

WHAT YOU'LL DO

- Use an activity sheet to discuss questions and fears kids have about AIDS
- Add a phrase to the Unit Affirmation Poster

WHAT YOU'LL NEED

- "Let's Talk About AIDS," Activity Sheet (page 31)
- Unit Affirmation Poster

3 Searching the Scripture (20 minutes)

WHAT YOU'LL DO

- Look at an object lesson which illustrates the treatment of lepers in Jesus' day
- Read an imaginary letter written by the leper to better understand his feelings about his sickness and healing

WHAT YOU'LL NEED

- Water
- Small, flat plate
- Bibles
- Food coloring
- Few drops of rubbing alcohol
- "Something to Write Home About," Activity Sheet (page 32)

4 Living the Lesson (5-10 minutes)

WHAT YOU'LL DO

- Use face paint and roleplay situations in which you can help AIDS patients

WHAT YOU'LL NEED

- Face paint

Setting the Stage (5-10 minutes)

Post the "Friendly Feud" strips in the front of the room with the "Welcome..." strip facing out so the kids can read it, and the others facing the wall so they can't be read.

As your kids arrive today, ask them to get ready to play "Friendly Feud" by making a list of the things kids their age fear the most. They should make their list as long as possible for use in the game. When everyone has arrived and had a few minutes to make a list, begin the game.

Divide the kids into two teams. **I have listed on the board three of the top fears that kids all over the country say they have. Each team will have a chance to guess what they think those fears are.** Now give each team a couple of minutes to compare their lists and choose five items that they think might be the correct answers. When the time is up, flip a coin to see which team goes first. Then, let that team say *one* of their fears. If it is correct, turn it over on the board and award points. If it is not correct, there is no penalty. Now ask the other team to guess. Continue alternating between the teams in this manner until all three answers have been revealed.

Introducing the Issue (20 minutes)

You kids are growing up today with some fears that we didn't have 20 or more years ago. You have just listed many of them, and they are all real fears and serious things to think about. Today, we are going to spend some time talking about one on the list, AIDS. This is a very emotional subject for many people and sometimes it's hard to sort out what is true and what is people's fears. Let's check out what we know about AIDS and be sure we all have the *right* information.

Distribute the activity sheet, "Let's Talk About AIDS" (page 31) and work through it together as a class. Be sure your kids have plenty of time to talk about any misconceptions they may have and they are allowed to openly express their fears. Then, share with them the real facts as you correct their misconceptions and allay their fears. Be aware that this session may stir strong feelings in your class, especially if any of your students know someone who has died of AIDS, have kids in their school who have AIDS, or have parents who have communicated strong fear and negative attitudes to their children.

1. Although your students may have heard this said, it is *not* true. In God's eyes sin is sin and He does not choose certain sins to punish over others. AIDS is a virus infection that can be spread only in certain ways. **What do you**

know about how AIDS is spread? Be sure they understand that it can *only* be spread in these ways: 1) Sexual contact with people who have the AIDS virus, 2) direct contact with contaminated blood, such as through blood transfusions and using contaminated needles, 3) an infected mother passing it to her unborn baby or through nursing it shortly after birth.

In God's eyes, a person with AIDS is *no* different than anyone else. We all do wrong things that separate us from God. We cannot shun people with AIDS because they are *bad*.

2. Experts now know for sure that AIDS cannot be spread through casual contact. **You *cannot* get AIDS from hugging, shaking hands with, or sitting next to a person with AIDS. You cannot get it from eating food prepared by someone who has it. It can *only* be contracted in one of the ways we just mentioned.**

It is important for your kids not to fear being with others, especially other kids, who have AIDS.

3. **Not anymore. At one time, people did get AIDS in that way. Today, doctors know how to test blood for the AIDS virus and they carefully check all donated blood before it is used.**

4. Your kids need to know that AIDS is spreading so quickly that it has been estimated that within a year or two, everyone in our country will know someone who has it or has died of it. Also, the epidemic is spreading among kids, and they will most likely have classmates with AIDS in the near future.

5. **AIDS patients are suffering in every way possible; physically from the disease, emotionally from being shunned, feared, and treated cruelly by everyone around them, and spiritually by coming to terms with their own deaths.** Help your kids know that they can be friends with those who have AIDS, and *not* be afraid of them. Reaching out in this way is a tremendous gift to the person with AIDS, his/her family, and to God. It will also help the person reaching out to grow, as well.

We need to take AIDS seriously. It is a real problem that affects all of us. However, we don't need to be afraid of it. By understanding how it is spread and living according to the teachings in God's Word, we eliminate the danger of getting it ourselves.

What does God's Word teach that would help protect us from the danger of getting AIDS? (No sex outside of marriage; take care of your bodies, no drugs.) **That frees us to care about those who do have it, and reach out to them with Jesus' love.**

Display the Unit Affirmation poster again this week, and review the information on it. Now let kids think of a phrase to add that summarizes today's discussion. Possibilities include, "by caring for others with AIDS," or, "by

believing correct information about AIDS."

Jesus gave us a great example of how to treat people with AIDS when He came into contact with people with another contagious disease.

Searching the Scriptures (20 minutes)

When Jesus lived on earth, the sickness that people feared most was leprosy. Here is an illustration of how people reacted to those suffering from this awful disease.

Start out the story by using this object lesson. Add food coloring to a small amount of water. Pour the water on a plate. Explain that this water represents healthy people. Add several drops of rubbing alcohol to the center of the water. The water will abruptly pull away from it, leaving a bare space in the center. The alcohol represents lepers.

What happened when the rubbing alcohol was added to the water? (It moved away from it.) **If the water and alcohol represent people, what do you think most people did when they met lepers?** (They avoided them, too.) This visual will return to normal shortly as the alcohol evaporates so you may want to repeat it for a greater effect.

Have your students turn in their Bibles to Mark 1:40-42 and choose a student to read aloud the verses. **Why did Jesus reach out and heal the leper?** (Because He felt compassion for the leper.) **What is compassion?** (A feeling of concern for another person.) **Let's read a letter that helps us imagine what the leper must have felt after he was healed.** Hand out copies of the "Something to Write Home About" activity sheet (page 32). Students can take turns reading the letter while the rest of the class follows along.

According to the letter, what did the leper have to give up when he got sick? (His home, family, work, friends, activities, everything.) **Where did he live?** (Alone or with others lepers outside the town.) **What did he have to do when he went out in public?** (Shout, "Unclean, unclean," to warn people he was coming; not touch anyone or get near them.) **Why did people treat lepers so harshly?** (They were afraid of catching leprosy from them.) **How does this compare with what happens when AIDS patients are with healthy people?** (They often react the same way; healthy people avoid people with AIDS.)

How do you think this kind of treatment made the leper feel? (Like an outcast; unhappy; sad; rejected.) **How do you think people with AIDS feel about the way people react to them?** (Like the leper.) Help your students understand that the way people reacted to these already sick people only made their illness harder to bear. It is hard to be in pain, fighting fatigue and infections all the time. When those struggles are compounded by trying to overcome rejection and hostility from other people, some patients feel it is almost too much to bear.

In the letter, the man was suprised by the way Jesus healed him. Why? (Jesus treated him as a person by showing love; He willingly reached out and touched this untouchable man.) When a person reaches out in love and compassion to someone with AIDS the first reaction by the patient is relief that someone really cares. Unfortunately, many times the people who care for these victims have no relationship with Jesus Christ. They can't give them the knowledge of God's love for them which gives them courage to face their suffering or any hope for a life after death.

How do you think the leper felt about Jesus after he was cured? (Grateful; thankful; loved Jesus; thought He was like God.) **What do you think he told other people about Jesus?** (He really cares for people; can heal any sickness; must be God's Son.) **How do you think his family felt about Jesus for healing their son and thus allowing him to come home again?** (Thankful; wanted to know more about Him; loved Him for what He did for their son.)

Recite the Unit Verse from I Timothy 6:18 together as a class. "Command them to do good, to be rich in good deeds, and to be generous and willing to share." **What are some ways you can obey this command and help people suffering from AIDS?** Give the kids an opportunity to respond. Help them think along the lines of: understanding; sympathy; support; comfort; sensitivity; kindness; gentleness; love; service. All these are Christian virtues and possible for us to share with AIDS victims.

When we ask Jesus to help us see people with AIDS as He does and fill us with His love then we can overcome our fears and prejudice. Only people who have a relationship with Jesus can share His love with others. At the present time we don't have the knowledge or ability to cure AIDS, but as Christians we can share the things that really matter in this life and the next.

Have your students help you choose a picture to accompany the heading "AIDS" and display it on your bulletin board or mural.

✓ Living the Lesson (5-10 minutes)

Explain to your students that you are going to let them have a chance to better understand people with AIDS. Divide the class into pairs. **Many AIDS patients suffer from a type of cancer which causes purple blotches like bruises to appear on their skin. We're going to make some of you look**

like AIDS patients today. Using the face paint and your finger make some spots on one kid from each pair. This kid is to act like an AIDS patient with possible problems of being tired, feverish, experiencing pain, etc. The remaining partner is to act like a healthy person.

Let kids take turns pantomiming different situations in which kids with AIDS interact with healthy kids. Some possibilities are: eating a meal together; sleeping next to each other at camp; washing hands in the washroom; playing a physical-contact game; attending the same Sunday school class. Pantomime a few of these situations as if the healthy person is fearful of getting the disease. Then have kids act out the remaining situations where the healthy person knows AIDS can't be caught by casual contact, using the same utensils, or even if an AIDS patient sneezes or coughs on you.

How did you *AIDS patients* feel in the first set of pantomimes? (Lonely; sad; left out; like you were a bad person.) **How did you feel in the second set of dramatizations?** (Thankful; almost like a normal person; grateful to be treated like a person, not a thing.) **Doing good means more than giving money. It means sharing feelings, friendships, love, and understanding. We will want to help people with AIDS because Jesus loves all of us.**

Ask volunteers to pray for victims of AIDS, asking God's help to reach out in compassion to share with them.

Let's Talk About AIDS

1. AIDS is a punishment from God on bad, sinful people. **YES NO**

2. AIDS is highly contagious and people who have it should be isolated from those who don't. **YES NO**

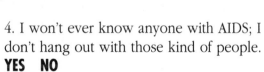

3. If I get sick and have to have a blood transfusion, could I get AIDS? **YES NO**

4. I won't ever know anyone with AIDS; I don't hang out with those kind of people. **YES NO**

5. AIDS patients need friends as much or more than anyone else. **YES NO**

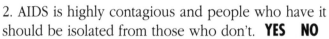

# Something to Write Home About

Dear Mother and Father,

I have great news! I'm well again. My leprosy is completely gone. I was healed in such a wonderful way. Let me tell you all about it.

You know how I hated to leave all of you when I discovered I had leprosy. But because people were afraid they would catch that terrible disease from me I couldn't live with you, be with my friends, go to parties or the synagogue, or do anything with other people. I wandered around alone for a long time. Everywhere I went I had to shout, "Unclean! Unclean!" People were always running to get out of my way. Finally I met some other lepers and joined them. We lived outside the town in crude huts made from branches. We had to beg for food. I was so lonely, sick, and sad. I prayed that God would help me.

Then one day I met a man who told me he had been sick once, too, but a man named Jesus had healed him. He was so happy he was telling everyone about it. "Would He heal me too?" I asked. "I know He can heal many kinds of sickness. Perhaps He would help a leper, too," the man answered.

After that, I kept thinking about this Jesus. Would He want to help me? I listened closely for any news about Jesus. One day all the townspeople were excited. Jesus was coming through our town that very day. This was my big chance to be healed. I felt that my prayers were about to be answered.

Soon the people began running down the road shouting, "He's coming! Jesus is coming!" A big crowd of people came into view. What should I do? Jesus would be gone if I didn't do something soon. I was desperate. I began to push my way through the crowd. People pulled away from me to keep from touching me. I knew I looked terrible. My hair was matted and dirty and my clothes were tattered. My hands were claw-shaped, my face was deformed, and I had spots all over my body. I heard a priest say, "How dare a leper come here? It's against the law to do this!" I kept going until finally I was in front of Jesus. I knew it was Him for He had the most loving face I've ever seen.

I dropped to my knees and said, "If You are willing, You can make me clean." Jesus looked directly into my eyes. He stretched out His hand toward me. Was He going to hit me or drive me away? Then it happened. Jesus touched me! "I am willing," He said. "Be clean." Immediately I felt well. The spots on my body were gone; my hands and my face were whole again. I can't begin to tell you how happy I was. It wasn't just that Jesus healed me. It was the way He did it. Jesus reached out and actually touched me, sick and ugly as I was. He treated me like a person. All the rest of my life I'll remember His tender touch. It was as if God reached out and touched me.

I'll be home soon, dear family. I can hardly wait to see all of you. Until then I send my love,

Benjamin

Lesson 4

Ganging Up 'n You

Aim: That your students will turn to God and Christian peer groups instead of violent gangs to satisfy their need of belonging.

Scripture: Proverbs 1:10-19

Unit Verse: Command them to do good, to be rich in good deeds, and to be generous and willing to share. I Timothy 6:18

Unit Affirmation: I CAN MAKE A DIFFERENCE!

 Planning Ahead

1. Make a caption entitled "GANGS" to add to the Unit Bulletin Board or Mural.
2. Cut out pictures from magazines or newspapers of groups of kids.
3. Contact someone who grows beautiful plants, someone who has a new puppy or kitten, and someone who has a new baby and ask them to be with you during SETTING THE STAGE, bringing their plant, puppy, and baby with them. Ask them to be prepared to talk with the kids in your class about what their item needs to grow healthy and strong.
4. Prepare four poster boards with the following headings: Healthy plants need . . . ; Healthy pets need . . . ; Healthy babies need . . . ; and, Healthy kids need . . .
5. Photocopy activity sheets (pages 39 and 40)–one for each student.

1 Setting the Stage (5-10 minutes)

WHAT YOU'LL DO

- Visit several stations to discover what living things need to thrive and be healthy

WHAT YOU'LL NEED

- A healthy plant, a puppy or kitten, a new baby, and four poster boards for the stations

2 Introducing the Issue (20 minutes)

WHAT YOU'LL DO

- Discuss the results of getting our needs met in unhealthy ways
- Use an activity sheet to identify the results of using gang membership to fulfill our need for belonging
- Add a phrase to the Unit Affirmation Poster

WHAT YOU'LL NEED

- It's Not Always As Good As It Looks," Activity Sheet, (page 39)
- Unit Affirmation Poster

3 Searching the Scriptures (20 minutes)

WHAT YOU'LL DO

- Present an object lesson to show how we become like the things we allow to influence us
- Read a paraphrase to find out what a wise father told his son about joining a violent gang

WHAT YOU'LL NEED

- Lump of modeling clay; a coin; a tree twig
- Bibles
- "Fatal Attachment," Activity Sheet (page 40)

4 Living the Lesson (5-10 minutes)

WHAT YOU'LL DO

- Make a list of tips on how to find good groups which will fulfill Juniors' need of belonging

WHAT YOU'LL NEED

- Chalkboard and chalk or sheet of newsprint and marker

 *Lesson 4*

Setting the Stage (5-10 minutes)

Have the four stations set up around the room when the kids arrive. Hang the poster boards so the kids will be able to write on them. Ask your guests to seat themselves near the appropriate poster board. (See Planning Ahead.) As the kids arrive, ask them to visit each station and talk with the person who is there. Based on their conversations, each student can each write o*ne* need s/he learned about on the poster.

Station yourself at the fourth poster (Healthy kids need . . .), **What do you need in order to grow strong and healthy?** Kids will probably respond with mostly phycsial needs. Encourage them to think of emotional and spiritual needs as well as physical ones. **What would a kid be like if s/he didn't receive love and attention? What would a kid be like if s/he didn't receive any encouragement? What would a kid be like if s/he didn't feel as if s/he belonged anywhere? What would a kid be like if s/he didn't know that God loved her/him and was caring for her/him?** Let the kids write their needs on the "Healthy Kids need . . ." poster.

Be sure to keep this moving, as they are likely to spend all their time with the puppy or kitten, and the baby. After about 10 minutes, gather the kids together.

Introducing the Issue (20 minutes)

As we have just seen, every living thing has needs that must be met in order for it to grow healthy and strong. What happens when these basic needs are *not* met? (They get sick or die; they are not as beautiful as they can be; etc.) **You have needs, too. What are they?** (Refer to the poster the kids created earlier.) **Are there other needs you have that we haven't listed yet?** (Be sure your list includes: belonging, love, respect, excitement, doing things well.)

What happens when kids don't get their needs met? (They can get sick and die; they will try to find some way of trying to meet their own needs.) **God's design is for kids to get their needs met by having families and other caring adults give them guidance, love, and all the physical things they need. However, sometimes parents and others don't provide what kids need. When that happens, kids sometimes go out looking for ways to get what they need.**

Explain that one of the biggest needs kids have is to feel they belong, and fit into a group of some kind. **What are some groups kids might join in**

order to feel as if they belong somewhere? (Some of the places kids go to find that belonging are positive; such as programs at church, community centers, or school. Others are negative; such as on the streets, or getting involved with the wrong group of friends.) **Many kids today are choosing to get involved with violent gangs as a way to get their needs met, especially the need to belong to a group and feel loved and accepted.**

Distribute copies of "It's Not As Good As It Looks," activity sheet (page 39). You will use the first half of the sheet to help kids realize that not everything in life turns out to be as good as it first appears, and the second half to show that a violent gang is *not* an appropriate way to satisfy their need for belonging.

Divide the kids into pairs. **Think of as many things as you can that seem good at first, but turn out to be disappointing or hurtful in the long run. Draw illustrations of one or two of your choices on the top half of your activity sheets.** After a few minutes, ask each pair to report on their discussion and show their illustrations. Comment on a few of their answers. **What is appealing about _____?** Answers will vary. **What needs are people trying to meet when they _____?** (Need to belong, need to feel important, need to be loved, need to be accepted, need to feel competent.)

Direct their attention to the bottom half of their sheets. **One thing that may seem good at first is joining a gang. What are the things about joining a gang that seem appealing?** (Gives you a place to belong, the way you dress gives you instant recognition on the street, brings respect and fear from non–group members, excitement, etc.) **Draw a picture or make a list of what is hurtful and destructive about being in a gang.** Kids may depict drugs, guns, knives, stealing, destroying property, jail, and even killing someone.

The bottom line is that joining a violent gang is one of those things that looks like it will give you a place to belong, respect, and excitement. But in reality, it could get you hooked on drugs, involved in breaking the law, arrested, and possibly even killed. You can find better ways to get your needs met! Stay away from gangs!

Display the Unit Affirmation poster. Since this is the last week of the unit, spend a few moments reviewing it. Remind your students that they are not too young or too small to make a difference in their world. As Christians, we can consider ourselves partners with God in caring for the hungry and homeless, using our possessions wisely, and reaching out to those suffering from AIDS. Have your students give suggestions of possible phrases to add to the last line. Choose one that says something like, "by staying away from violent gangs."

Did you know that God's Word talks about joining gangs? Let's see what Solomon wrote to his son in the Book of Proverbs.

Lesson 4

 # Searching the Scriptures (20 minutes)

Have your students turn to Proverbs 1:10-19 and follow along in their Bibles as you read these verses. **What was Solomon warning his son about?** (Avoiding violent people.) **Why do you think Solomon warned his son about violent people?** (He didn't want his son to be influenced by their violence; he knew that violence would only lead to trouble for his son.)

What happens when you hang around with people that resort to violence? Your students will probably mention that they may be influenced to be violent, too. To emphasize this fact, show your students the lump of clay. **Clay takes on the shape of whatever pushes against it. I can squeeze it with my hand into a ball or roll in between my hands like a snake, press a coin or twig in it, and the clay takes on the likeness of that thing. When the clay hardens it keeps the image of whatever shaped it.**

Discuss how kids are like the clay. Their behavior becomes molded by that of the groups they join. When they join a positive group they act in helpful, law-abiding ways. If they join groups that use violence they end up breaking laws and committing hurtful crimes. That is why it is important they avoid gangs that resort to violence and crime.

Hand out "Fatal Attachment," activity sheet (page 40). **Here is a paraphrase of the Bible passage we just read. In other words, it has been put into more modern language. It gives a clear description of the kinds of gangs to avoid.** Read the introductory paragraph at the top of the page and have a volunteer read the paraphrase.

What are some of the violent actions mentioned here? (Beating people up; mugging; theft; shoplifting; selling stolen property; abusing liquor and/or drugs; gang fights; murder.) Kids often join gangs not only for the sense of belonging but also for the excitement of group activities. Violent gangs offer an element of risk, thrill, and excitement but you need to help your students realize that the results of those activities are destructive to both the victims and the perpetrators.

How do you think victims feel after they have been attacked? (Afraid; in pain; angry.) **Have any of you had something stolen? How did you feel about it?** Probably at least one or more of your students has experienced this or knows of someone else who has. Have them share about it. It is a humiliating affront to have personal effects stolen from our homes, cars, or lockers.

Do you agree or disagree with this statement: Shoplifting is okay. You don't hurt anyone when you steal from a big store. You may have some disagreements here due to lack of knowledge of the facts. Explain that merchandise is generally covered by insurance but such losses have to be made up by the companies. This results in higher costs to the store for coverage and is eventually passed on to the customers who pay more for items purchased.

Do the results of these gang crimes seem like benefits to the victims? (No.) Help your students to understand that because of these harmful results, law enforcement becomes more strict and lawbreakers end up paying a higher cost for their crimes in fines or jail sentences.

According to the paraphrase, things are shared equally. What are the benefits of sharing things equally? Kids need to have a sense of belonging and by sharing equally they get it. There are many things that they need to share. Love, friendship, trust, self-esteem, and their Christian faith are all things that fit in this category. But there are also some things they need to avoid sharing with others. Discuss some of these. **What consequences might there be if the things shared are alcohol and other drugs?** (Addiction; substance abuse; even death.) **What could be the outcome of sharing in a gang war?** (Members can get hurt or killed; bystanders can get injured; acts of revenge and feuds are prolonged or intensified.) Point out that sharing equally in injuries or death isn't much of a benefit.

What do you think the paraphrase meant by comparing trying to catch birds in a net with members of violent gangs laying a booby trap for themselves? Allow your students some time to think this out on their own before you offer them any insight. Having an adult tell them that it is wrong to carry out violent acts and crimes is not as strong a deterrent as having them think the whole thing through from instigation to result. When they reason out for themselves that the momentary pleasures and thrills of violence aren't worth the possibilities of jail, injuries, or death, then they have a stronger foundation for making wise judgments about the groups they join.

✔ Living the Lesson (5-10 minutes)

Recite together the Unit Verse from I Timothy 6:18. "Command them to do good, to be rich in good deeds, and to be generous and willing to share." **This verse seems to refer to the kind of group that is directly opposite to the one we just studied about in Proverbs.**

Direct your students' attention to the bottom of their activity sheets. **If you were going to design a *good* gang, what would be some beneficial things to include in it?** Have your kids work on this activity individually or in pairs. After doing this, they can discuss their creations and help you design an *ideal* gang which will fulfill their need of belonging. Some qualities that could be included are: friendliness; equal treatment for every member; trust; loyalty to

one another and the group; encouragement; caring for members when they have problems; helping members to be the very best they can be; respecting the rights of others. List these characteristics on your chalkboard or a sheet of newsprint.

What are some gangs/groups like this? Encourage your students to think of your class as one place their needs can be filled. Other possibilities could be groups where they would have interaction with Christian peers such as youth groups, church kids' clubs; sports teams; musical or drama clubs. If your church or area doesn't have any of these kinds of gangs for Juniors, perhaps now is the time to provide one for them.

By being members of this kind of a gang it is much easier to obey the command in our Unit Verse. Guide your kids to realize that members of that kind of a group encourage and help each other to do good things. They find their riches in good deeds done for others, not stolen property. The things they have to share with each other generously are helpful things that build one another up and benefit nonmembers as well as themselves.

Let your students help you pick a picture to illustrate the caption "Gangs" and display both items on the bulletin board or mural.

Close class with a group heart prayer. Kids all hold hands but instead of standing in a circle, have them form a heart. Close by praying for each other as members of God's "gang" or family.

Not Always As Good As It Looks ✓

Things are not always what they seem to be . . .

 take a closer look and you'll see . . .

Gangs are not always what they seem to be . . .

 take a closer look and you'll see . . .

✔ Fatal Attachment

Solomon was the wisest man in the world. He loved his son and wanted only the best for him. He told his son how to avoid the dangers of joining gangs that use violence. Here is a paraphrase of what Solomon said in Proverbs 1:10-19:

Kids, if tough members of bad gangs want you to join them in committing crimes, don't do it.

They might say, "Come with us. Let's hide in the alley and beat somebody up just for fun. We can mug someone and take their money. Let's break into some houses and cars and steal things. We'll get tape decks, boom boxes, jewelry, clothes, guns, car parts, and lots of other things. We can even do some shoplifting. It doesn't hurt anybody, because the stores have insurance that pays for stolen stuff. We can sell what we steal or keep it for ourselves. If you join our gang we'll split everything we get equally with you.

When we have liquor or drugs you can have some, too. We'll fight any other gangs that try to take over our territory. We might even kill someone. But you'll be one of us and we take care of each other.

Kids, don't join those kind of gangs. Don't do the things they do or get involved with them at all. They are quick to turn to violence and crime. They run to a fight and hurt or kill each other.

If someone is going to catch birds, he doesn't spread out a net where the birds can see it because then the birds would stay away. Members of bad gangs are more stupid than birds. They are laying a booby trap for themselves because violence only causes more violence. People who choose to commit crimes end up in jail. Kids who hurt and kill others end up getting killed.

"CREATE A GANG" Use the space below to write some qualities you would want in a group if you were going to design a gang that would be fun for kids to join and helpful for its members.

Service Projects for Problems in Society

In addition to the projects listed in these lessons your class or church can also serve in the following ways:

 ## The Hungry

1. Visit a food shelf to see how people get food and find out needed items
2. Help distribute or pack items at a food shelf
3. Help deliver "Meals on Wheels"
4. Notify church members you will have a scavenger hunt of needed food items so they can be prepared to donate them when teams show up
5. Kidnap your pastor, youth leader, etc., and have church members contribute food items or money to be used for them as the ransom money

 ## The Homeless

1. Adopt a homeless brother/sister/family and bring them home with you for visits or take them on family outings with you
2. Trim a Christmas tree with cardboard decorations each listing a project or item and the amount of money needed for it. People can choose which one they want to do and consider it their Christmas gift to Jesus
3. Visit residents at nursing homes. Call nursing home residents to congratulate them on birthdays, holidays, or just to talk to them; do errands, shop, write letters for nursing home residents; put on a special program for a nursing home; adopt a grandparent from a nursing home and give him or her special attention throughout the year; bring a pet for a visit so it can be enjoyed by nursing home residents
4. Sponsor a child in a foreign country
5. Show movies for migrant families and/or refugee groups in their own language or give out tracts or Scripture in their language

 ## Poverty and Materialism

1. Recycle used or leftover Sunday school or VBS materials for needy churches
2. Repair and recycle used toys, games, entertainment items such as radios or TVs
3. Go without extras you don't need and give the money to projects to benefit the need (this can include clothing, entertainment, and food items)

 ## Aids

1. Send a class letter to a sick person
2. Offer to do small chores or errands for someone with AIDS. Writing letters, shopping, helping take care of pets, or dusting all become difficult for these people
3. Visit patients and chat for a brief time
4. Bring small "happy" gifts such as balloons, puzzles, magazines, toys
5. Call them on the telephone. Let them know you care about them and are praying for them

 ## Gangs, Crime, and Violence

1. Show your local police department your appreciation by bringing a special treat for officers
2. Invite an officer to your group to share concerns, warnings, etc. Let this be an informal time to just get acquainted with them
3. Have a special game time, picnic, party where you invite kids outside your church to come and get acquainted with the youth activities at your church
4. Start a special club or "good" gang where kids can enjoy activities together and feel they belong

Picking and Choosing

Children today are faced with more difficult choices than at any other time in our history. It is not uncommon for your Juniors to be facing decisions regarding the use of alcohol and other drugs, beginning experimentation with sex, and choosing between parents in custody battles. Making choices such as these is particularly stressful and confusing for Juniors, especially when you consider that parents, teachers, peers, and the media often tell them very different things about what is right and wrong.

In this unit, your students will learn the importance of good decision making, and how every choice they make has an impact on many other areas of their lives. Through the use of the Unit Verse and the Unit Affirmation, they will discover two keys to wise decision making:

1. Our relationship to God and knowledge of His Word. Living as God's children and following biblical principles is our most valuable resource for making wise choices.

2. Learning to *think* before we choose. Avoiding impulsive decision making is a result of thinking about all available options, the consequences of each option, including measuring it against the standards of God's Word, and whether or not to ask a trusted adult for help.

Although you will most likely not be present when your students face the difficult decisions of their lives, you can know that you will be empowering them to make wise choices as you teach them the skills in this unit.

✔ Making Choices Overview

Unit Verse: Psalm 111:10–The fear of the Lord is the beginning of wisdom; all who follow his precepts have good understanding.

Unit Affirmation: I CAN THINK BEFORE I CHOOSE!

LESSON	TITLE	OBJECTIVE	SCRIPTURE BASE
Lesson #1	Decisions, Decisions, Decisions	That your students will learn that life is a series of choices that affects the direction their lives take.	Matthew 25:1-10
Lesson #2	An Unchanging Guide	That your students will acknowledge God's Word as an unchanging standard and use it to help them make choices.	Matthew 7:24-27; II Timothy 3:16, 17
Lesson #3	Who You Gonna Call?	That your students will identify wise people who can help them make decisions and call upon when needed.	Exodus 18:13-26
Lesson #4	I Challenge You!	That your students will wisely choose to follow God's way.	Esther 4:1-16; 7:1-4; 8:7, 8, 16, 17

Partners

For the next few weeks your junior-age child will be part of a group learning about Making Choices. Partners is a planned parent piece to keep you informed of what will be taught during this exciting series.

PREVIEW...
Making Wise Choices

Being a parent can be scary! Each day, when you send your children out the door to school or to play, you know they will be exposed to a wide variety of influences over which you often have little control. In our society today, it is pretty much taken for granted that your children will receive differing messages as to what is right and wrong from teachers, peers, coaches, media, and a host of others who have a part in shaping their lives. As Christian parents, we also know that in America many of the traditional biblical values we hold dear are no longer generally accepted throughout our society. So, you may be like many parents today who feel anxious about the difficult choices your children are

confronted with every day. At those moments, when you are not there to guide them, will your children know what to do? In this unit on making wise choices, your children will be learning key principles they can use to make wise choices, especially during those times when it may seem particularly hard to know what to do. Certainly, no one can guarantee that your children will always make the wisest choice in every situation. However, we can prepare them to face difficult choices by teaching them to apply basic decision-making skills to any situation in which they may find themselves. Although we may not always be able to protect our children from the difficult decisions real life throws at them, we can rest easier knowing we have armed them with good decision-making skills they can use when we cannot be there to guide them.

PRINCIPLES...
Making Wise Choices
1. A RELATIONSHIP TO GOD AND FOLLOWING THE TEACHINGS OF HIS WORD

ARE THE BEST SOURCES FOR MAKING WISE CHOICES.

This principle is being taught each week through the Unit Verse, Psalm 111:10: The fear of the Lord is the beginning of wisdom; all who follow his precepts have good understanding.

As our children grow up in a world that is changing all the time, they need to know there is a source of security and wisdom that does *not* change. In our world today, the best news is still the Good News that Jesus calls children to Himself. As parents and teachers, it is our job to open the way for our kids to come to Him and to help them see that Jesus is always present and can be called on to help in even their most difficult decision-making times.

But there is more! In a time when many around them are saying, "Do whatever you feel is right," and everyone has a different opinion about what that means, children need the security of knowing there is a consistent standard of right and wrong that can be learned and trusted, and that standard is found in God's Word. In many ways, the most valuable skill we can offer our children is the skill of applying God's Word to the choices they make each day.

2. MAKING WISE CHOICES TAKES TIME AND CAREFUL THOUGHT.

Each week during this unit, your kids will be focusing on this principle as they talk about the Unit Affirmation: **I CAN THINK BEFORE I CHOOSE!** They will be learning to stop and think about these things:

• What are the consequences of each choice? Once we stop to think about our choices, we can begin to sort them out by thinking about what would happen if we followed through on each one.

• What are my options in this situation? Many times, poor choices are made simply because we didn't stop long enough to think through all the possibilities open to us.

• What does God's Word say about this situation? Again, using God's Word as a guide for choosing a course of action is a valuable skill for all of us.

• Do I need help making this choice? Children need to learn that it is OK to ask for help when we need it! Paying attention to the signals our bodies and emotions give us will help us know when it is time to ask for help!

Learning to **THINK BEFORE WE CHOOSE** helps us be clear and creative about the choices we make every day!

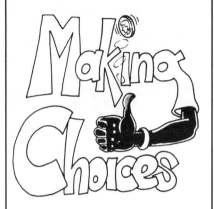

PRACTICE...
Making Wise Choices

You can reinforce what your children are learning in this unit by doing one or more of these at-home activities:

1. HIDE GOD'S WORD IN YOUR HEARTS.

Learn the Unit Verse together as a family. Write the verse out on a 3" x 5" card and keep it on or near your kitchen table. During mealtimes, read the verse together several times each day. Make a game of it by asking the youngest person in the family to say the first word of the verse, the next youngest to say the next word, etc. Continue until the verse has been said correctly. If someone misses a word, start over from the beginning of the verse. Once you have memorized Psalm 111:10, do the same thing with James 1:5, another important verse for making wise choices.

2. AFFIRMATION CARDS

Start with four 3" x 5" cards. On one side of each card write, **I CAN THINK BEFORE I CHOOSE!** On the other side, write one of the following phrases:

• Think about the consequences of your choice
• Think about all your options
• Think about how God's Word can help you choose
• Do you need to ask for help?

Keep these cards close at hand. As your children face choices in their lives, offer them the affirmation cards as reminders to use good decision-making skills. For instance, if your child reports at suppertime that she got invited to a party on Friday night, and therefore wants to back out of her agreement to spend the night at another friend's house, you could hand her the affirmation cards and ask her to use them to guide her as she thinks about what she should do.

Affirmation cards can be used in lots of ways. They can be tucked into children's backpacks to be used during those times when you cannot be with them. Or, you can learn good decision-making skills as a family by using the affirmation cards to make a family decision. For instance, if your family is in conflict over TV viewing rules, get out the affirmation cards and work through each one before deciding on the final rules.

Decisions, Decisions, Decisions!

Aim: That your students will learn that life is a series of choices that affects the direction their lives take.

Scripture: Matthew 25:1-10

Unit Verse: The fear of the Lord is the beginning of wisdom; all who follow his precepts have good understanding. Psalm 111:10

Unit Affirmation: I CAN THINK BEFORE I CHOOSE!

Planning Ahead

1. Prepare a set of cards (approximately 6" x 6") that spell out the phrase, "I CAN THINK BEFORE I CHOOSE," placing only one letter on each card. Pin these to a bulletin board (or tape them to the wall) in the correct order, but with the letters facing the wall so that they cannot be seen.
2. Wrap five or six gifts. Make these various sizes, shapes, and wrappings. Place items you know the kids will *not* like (a can of spinach, an empty candy wrapper, a small puzzle with half the pieces missing, etc.) in the biggest and most attractively wrapped packages. Place items you know the kids WILL like (a real candy bar, a gift certificate for McDonald's® a small toy, etc.) in the smaller, plainer boxes. Then, place one dollar in the smallest box and wrap it with newspaper and masking tape.
3. Prepare the Unit Affirmation Poster by writing I CAN THINK BEFORE I CHOOSE! on the top of a large poster board.
4. Fasten a large piece of shelf paper to a wall before class. Have writing materials available for students to use to make a graffiti wall.
5. Photocopy activity sheets (pages 51 and 52)—one for each student.

1 | Setting the Stage (5-10 minutes)

WHAT YOU'LL DO

- Play a game to discover the Unit Affirmation

WHAT YOU'LL NEED

- Letter cards that spell out the Unit Affirmation

2 | Introducing the Issue (20 minutes)

WHAT YOU'LL DO

- Participate in a gift exchange and use an activity sheet to discover that choices have consequences
- Introduce the Unit Affirmation Poster

WHAT YOU'LL NEED

- A number of gift packages prepared in advance (see instructions for details)
- A pair of dice or a spinner
- "Be Careful What You Choose!" Activity Sheet (page 51)
- Unit Affirmation Poster, prepared in advance

3 | Searching the Scriptures (20 minutes)

WHAT YOU'LL DO

- Solve a mystery to discover some of the differences between wise and foolish choices

WHAT YOU'LL NEED

- Bibles
- "The Fascinating Case of the Five Failing Flames," Activity Sheet (page 52)

4 | Living the Lesson (5-10 minutes)

WHAT YOU'LL DO

- Practice making choices and discuss the wisdom of each
- Participate in a brief candlelight prayer service

WHAT YOU'LL NEED

- Matches, small candles—one for yourself and each student

Lesson 1

 # Setting the Stage (5-10 minutes)

As your students arrive, talk with them about how their weeks have gone. Ask them questions that focus on choices they made with what to do with their time after school or on the weekend. Ask about choices they made regarding what to do with their friends. Use the word choose and choices throughout the conversation. Help them to see some of the consequences of their choices–positive and negative.

When you think all of your kids have arrived, draw their attention to the cards you have fixed on the bulletin board or wall and introduce the game to them. **We're going to begin today by playing a game where we need to choose letters in order to guess a phrase.** Let kids take turns guessing a letter. If the letter is in the phrase, turn the card(s) over so they can be read. Continue letting students take turns guessing letters until someone guesses what the phrase says.

Ask students to comment on what they think the phrase means. Allow a few students to share their ideas. **We are starting a new unit today about making choices. It's an important unit because some of the choices we will be making will have consequences we will need to live with all our lives. This phrase, "I CAN THINK BEFORE I CHOOSE," tells us an important truth to remember about making good choices. We will be learning more about what that all means as we go along.**

 # Introducing the Issue (20 minutes)

Let's give you a chance to practice making some choices! This activity will prepare your students for a discussion of one reason we need to think about our choices–namely, often our first inclination when making a decision is not necessarily the best one.

To play the game, sit everyone in a circle around a table or on the floor, and place the gifts you have previously wrapped in the middle. Instruct the kids that they will each have a turn to throw the dice (or spin a spinner) and that anyone who rolls doubles (or spins a certain number) may choose a gift, but not open it. They may choose any gift at anytime, even if someone else has already chosen it. Play the game for about seven or eight minutes.

After you call time, ask those who are holding gifts to tell the class why they wanted that particular gift, and to make a guess as to what is inside. Then, allow them to open the gifts. **What did you get?** Allow responses. **Did you make a good choice?** Some will think so; others will not. **Would you make** the same choice again, if you could do it over? What might you think about next time?

We have just played a game in which we had to make some choices. Most of us decided which gifts we wanted by looking at how big or attractive the gift was. However, when we opened the gifts, we discovered that those criteria did not necessarily help us make the best choices.

Explain that that is the way it is with making all kinds of decisions. Sometimes we choose to do something for what may seem like a good reason at the time, but we find out later that it was not such a wise choice after all.

OPTIONAL: Share a time from your life when you made a choice that turned out to be a poor choice. Explain the choice and the consequences.

Can you think of a time you made a choice that turned out to be an unwise choice? What were the consequences of your decision that were hard to live with? (Possibilities may include: cheating on a test and losing your teacher's trust; not cleaning your room when asked to and forfeiting your allowance or being grounded; buying something that turned out to be a waste of money and being short on money for something else, etc.)

What are some things you may be tempted to choose because they look appealing, but may actually be poor choices? (Possibilities may include: doing something we know is wrong so others will accept us; watching certain TV shows or movies that we know are "trash in disguise" or will give us nightmares; eating too much junk food; etc.)

Distribute the "Be Careful What You Choose," activity sheet (page 51). Have a student read aloud the first choice. What might be some of the consequences of this choice? Allow the students to answer and complete their papers as a class. Continue this for each of the choices. We have been talking about how easy it is to let first impressions determine our choices, and how that does *not* always lead us to make the best decisions. When we make poor choices, we have to live with the consequences of our choice. Learning how to think ahead and make wise choices is an important skill that we will be learning more about in the weeks ahead.

Display the Unit Affirmation Poster where everyone can see it and you can easily write on it. Ask the class to read it aloud together. There are many things for us to think about before we choose. What did we talk about today that tells us one thing we must think about before we make our choices? Let students share their ideas. Conclude the discussion by writing the word, "Consequences," under the affirmation on the poster. Remind the kids

that the first step in making good choices is to stop and think about the *consequences* of the choice they are about to make. **We do this by stopping for a moment to ask ourselves, "What is going to happen as a result of what I have just decided to do? Am I going to feel good about what will come next?" Remember, don't choose first impressions . . . YOU CAN THINK ABOUT THE CONSEQUENCES BEFORE YOU CHOOSE!**

Searching the Scriptures (20 minutes)

Help your students to see that when you don't think about possible outcomes before you make a decision you often make foolish mistakes that end in trouble. **There is a story in the Bible that shows us an example of not thinking ahead.** Have students open their Bibles to Matthew 25:1-10 and follow along as you read the parable of the ten young girls. **Who are the two groups of girls Jesus tells about?** (The wise girls and foolish girls.) **What did the foolish girls do or not do to make them foolish?** (Failed to bring oil; failed to think ahead.)

Now, let's see how good you are at thinking ahead. I'm going to give you an opportunity to become detectives. Your job is to help Detective Vic Tracy and his associate, Willie Catchem, with a baffling mystery, the Case of the Five Failing Flames.

Hand out "The Case of the Five Failing Flames" activity sheet (page 52). This is a humorous takeoff on the Bible parable of the ten young girls. Because of the way it is written, it is a sort of tongue twister. Let your students take turns reading it. Have fun and be ready for some laughs! Allow time to get over the giggles before trying to discuss the truths hidden within the story.

What are some of the things that all ten girls had in common? (All were invited; all started out with lamps and oil; all fell asleep; all relit their lamps.) **What was the main difference between the five wise and five foolish girls?** (Five wise thought ahead to more than one result and planned for changes; other five only considered that they had enough for normal time period, didn't allow for any variations.)

What was the first thing the five foolish friends did when they realized they didn't have enough oil? (They tried to borrow some from their friends.) **Have you ever tried to get your friends to help you out of tight spots when you've made poor choices? Did your friends help you out? How do you think they feel when you put them on the spot like that?** Let volunteers share their experiences.

When the foolish friends couldn't get their wise friends to help them,

what did the foolish girls do? (They started making excuses and blaming other people for their troubles.) **What excuses might the five foolish friends have given?** (It wasn't their fault; if the other girls had really been their friends and shared with them they wouldn't have been in trouble; if the host had been on time things would have turned out all right; the stores were closed and they couldn't buy oil.) Discuss how blaming others doesn't help anyone. Instead it starts arguments and breaks up friendships. Each person needs to be responsible for his or her own actions and choices.

What was the result of the girls' foolish choice? (They missed out on the party.) **How could they have avoided this outcome?** (By thinking ahead to what might happen to change the situation and preparing for those changes in advance.) Pursue the decision-making process further by discussing some other possible results of this foolish choice. **What do you think happened to the friendship between the wise and foolish girls? How do you think the host felt about asking the girls to another party? What do you think the other guests thought about the girls after that evening?** Point out that all these potential consequences could have been avoided by simply thinking ahead before making a final choice. Learning through experience alone can truly be learning the hard way!

How can we avoid making the same kind of mistakes these girls did? (Think through the problem and try to anticipate what the results of choices might be before we actually make the decision.)

Introduce the Unit Verse, "The fear of the Lord is the beginning of wisdom; all who follow his precepts have good understanding." (Psalm 111:10) **The key word here is "beginning." If you want or need wisdom, you must start at the beginning. What is the beginning?** (The fear of the Lord.) Encourage your class to see that some better words for fear as it is meant in this verse are reverence or respect. You can paraphrase the verse something like this: **God knows everything. He has thought ahead and knows how to avoid problems and mistakes. If I want to make a wise choice, I must start by respecting Him and seeking His advice. If I rush ahead and make choices based on my wisdom alone, I'm likely to make foolish decisions which end in mistakes.**

On the shelf paper you have hung, have your kids make a graffiti wall by writing statements or drawing pictures that illustrate the principles taught throughout this unit. Allow them to be as creative and humorous as possible. Some examples for today are: Plan ahead, it wasn't raining when Noah built the ark; Look before you leap; Hasty choices cause foolish mistakes. You will be adding to the graffiti throughout this unit. Caution: be careful with writing materials so the wall behind the paper isn't marked up also!

✓ **Living the Lesson** (5-10 minutes)

Let your students try applying today's biblical principle. Give them two or three situations where they must make a decision. Allow a brief time to think about possible results. Discuss whether the choices in the situations were wise or foolish. **What possible consequences did these kids fail to think about? What things should you look out for if you were faced with a similar problem?** Point out that in each case there are both short- and long-range results. **How would knowing God's Word help make such decisions easier?**

Some examples of situations are:

• Your friend says, "We have a substitute teacher today. I heard she isn't taking roll. Let's skip out and go to the mall."

• You have been told to stay home while your parents are out. You're really bored. You could take your bike and ride down the highway to visit your friend. If you hurry, your parents won't know you've been gone.

• You are walking home after school with your friend. S/he asks to borrow your spelling paper to copy it.

• You are angry at your neighbor because he accused you of something you didn't do. His car is parked in his driveway. You feel like sneaking over and letting the air out of his tires.

Close with a candlelight prayer service. Use sentence prayers to ask God's guidance, forgiveness for poor choices, or thanks for help in making wise choices. Pass out the candles and darken the room. Light your candle and pray. Then light the candle of the person on your right. That student prays and lights the candle of the person on his/her right. Proceed until everyone has prayed and holds a lighted candle.

Be Careful What You Choose

All of our choices have consequences. What might happen as a consequence of each of these choices?

CHOICE #1: You were sick two days this week and so didn't learn your spelling words. You choose to cheat on the test.

CONSEQUENCES:_____

_____

_____

_____

_____

_____

_____

_____

CHOICE #2: It's Saturday and your room is a mess. You choose to clean it up before your mom asks you to!

CONSEQUENCES:_____

_____

_____

_____

_____

_____

_____

CHOICE #3: You come home from school and know no one will be home until 5:30. You are hungry, so you eat half a bag of chips, lots of M&Ms, the last piece of chocolate cake, and drink a can of Coke.

CONSEQUENCES:_____

_____

_____

_____

_____

_____

_____

'The Fascinating Case of the Five Failing Flames'

Fearless Vic Tracy and his faithful fellow cop Willie Catchem frowned as they studied the file papers before them. "Found anything yet, Tracy?" Willie asked. "I'm feeling frustrated this time."

"First, let's face the facts," Tracy answered. "Ten females, all friends of this fellow are invited to a fiesta. Faithfully they bring the functioning lamps requested and sit down to await his arrival. Some unforeseen fate delays the fellow and the friends fall asleep. Finally, folks wake them at midnight and call them to come meet him. The females, with fleet fingers, fix their lamps by trimming the wicks and adding fire to them. Fanning them furiously, the flames flare fast and the girls, fun-loving, frolicky, and fond of food are ready to join the festival. And that's when it happens, Willie."

"Five of their flames fade and fail. But why, Tracy? What foul felon would commit such a crime? And why would he fix it so only half the lamps fizzled?" Willie fumbled, falteringly.

"Why indeed? According to the statements taken, the five females whose flames blazed favorably brought along extra fuel for them."

"I guess that's why you could say that Wanda, Wendy, Whitney, Winnie, and Wilona were wise, right, Tracy? But what about the other five females—Freda, Frances, Fritzi, Fern, and Flora, the ones who found their flames flickering and faltering? They were forced to flee and got left behind. It says here they found fault with their friends and feel this fellow was unfair."

"It sounds fishy to me, Willie. You're forgetting that tempers can flare furiously when folks are forced to see the folly of their choices. There's a flaw in the flow of the reasoning of these unfortunate five. They freely admit they didn't consider any unforeseen forces that might have changed their situation. Their fallacy lies in faulty thinking. Even a furnace will go out if it runs out of fuel."

"What do you mean, Tracy? What fallacy made the fading flames fail?"

"These five fussers didn't think ahead, Willie. They were so eager to fleet-foot it to the feast they didn't fortify their lamps with extra fuel. When the flames floundered, they figured they could fool their friends into furnishing them with a fresh flow. When that failed, they were forced to flee to the nearest store to obtain more fuel. While they were gone, this fellow came and their five wise friends followed him into the fiesta without them. Now these five are finding fault."

"What about the finger pointing at the fellow and friends? A fraud?"

"Pure fiction, Willie. A fable fabricated by five fidgeters who refused to 'fess up that they made a foolish choice."

"You mean the flop was their own fault? They failed to think ahead?"

"Fantastically stated, Willie. Before forging ahead furiously, it is fundamental that you found your decision on firm footing and consider future outcomes. In this instance it was a foolish choice that caused the five to forfeit a fabulous feast. Case finished." Tracy flipped the file folder to Willie and reached for his favorite fedora.

"What should I do with this, Tracy? File it under 'Foolish?'"

"Fine, my favorite friend." Tracy flashed his famous smile and added, "Let's hope that in the future, Freda, Frances, Fritzi, Fern, and Flora will make wise choices like their friends, Wanda, Wendy, Whitney, Winnie, and Wilona."

Willie filed the folder, flipped the drawer shut, flicked the light off and finally followed Tracy from the room.

Activity Sheet by Bev Gundersen © 1991 David C. Cook Publishing Co. Permission granted to reproduce for classroom use only.

Lesson 2

An Unchanging Guide

Aim: That your students will acknowledge God's Word as an unchanging standard and use it to help them make choices.

Scripture: Matthew 7:24-27; II Timothy 3:16, 17

Unit Verse: The fear of the Lord is the beginning of wisdom; all who follow his precepts have good understanding. Psalm 111:10

Unit Affirmation: I CAN THINK BEFORE I CHOOSE!

 **Planning Ahead**

1. Photocopy activity sheets (pages 59 and 60)–one for each student

1 Setting the Stage (5-10 minutes)

WHAT YOU'LL DO

- Use an activity sheet to introduce the concept of identifying all available options
- Observe and discuss a short skit illustrating the process of thinking about options

WHAT YOU'LL NEED

- "How Many Choices Can I Find?" Activity Sheet (page 59)
- A watch with a second hand
- 2 small prizes

2 Introducing the Issue (20 minutes)

WHAT YOU'LL DO

- Brainstorm possible options to real-life situations
- Add two phrases to the Unit Affirmation Poster

WHAT YOU'LL NEED

- A sleeping bag, pillow, and an alarm clock for the skit, "Wake Up, Susie"
- Unit Affirmation Poster from last week

3 Searching the Scriptures (20 minutes)

WHAT YOU'LL DO

- Observe an object lesson to better understand God's Word is a valuable standard to help them make wise decisions
- Build something out of teacher-provided materials

WHAT YOU'LL NEED

- 4 cups: ordinary, decorative, large, measuring cup
- Bibles
- Toothpicks or decks of game cards
- Children's building blocks

4 Living the Lesson (5-10 minutes)

WHAT YOU'LL DO

- Practice using God's Word to make wise choices

WHAT YOU'LL NEED

- "Look It Up" Activity Sheet (page 60)

Setting the Stage (5-10 minutes)

Before your students arrive, set out copies of the "How Many Choices Can I Find?" activity sheet (page 59). As kids come into the room, pair them off and ask them to get started on writing their possibilities for how to spend their day off school. Instruct them that this is a game, and the pair that comes up with the most options for how they can spend their free day will be the winners. When all have arrived and had a few minutes to make a list, call time. Then, introduce today's theme. **Have you ever gotten up on a free day, or on a summer day and said, "I'm bored; there's nothing to do!"? Usually, when we approach a day with that attitude, we spend the rest of the day being bored! The problem, however, isn't with the day; it's because we never took the time to think carefully about all the options available to us. Let's see how many alternatives you came up with today.**

Review the lists that were made, encouraging those who showed creativity in coming up with many diverse possibilities. Congratulate the pair with the longest list and award a small prize. Then, tell kids that they will have one more chance to create an options list. This time, you will time them to see which pair can create the longest and most creative list in exactly three minutes! Using a watch with a second hand, allow students to work on the second half of the page. Call time after three minutes, and once again compare lists. Award a small prize to the winning pair. **Thinking about all the options we have can be fun. It helps us to remember that we have many possible alternatives when we need to make a choice.**

Introducing the Issue (20 minutes)

Let's look at Susie's options when she needs to make a decision first thing in the morning. You will need another person to help you with this skit. If possible, seat children in a circle on the floor, with "Susie" lying in a sleeping bag in the middle. If your room is small and you must be seated around a table, Susie can be resting her head on the table. The following skit may be photocopied for use in the classroom only.

TEACHER: This is Susie. She got to bed late last night, so I don't think she will be too happy when this alarm goes off. (Turn it on and place it by Susie's ear.) There it goes now. Let's see what happens.

SUSIE: (Groans; reaches for it "sleepily"; knocks it over; turns it off and goes back to sleep.)

TEACHER: Hey, Susie! You can't go back to sleep! Your mom is going to yell at you any moment, and if you don't get going, you'll be late for school.

SUSIE: I don't care, I'm *tired!* I shouldn't a stayed up watching that dumb movie last night . . . *Hey!* who are you and what are you doing in my bedroom?? (Sits up and sees all the kids.) UGH! What are all of *them* doing in my bedroom?

TEACHER: Well, we're learning about how to make good choices, and since you have one to make right now, we thought we'd pop in and see what we can learn from you!

SUSIE: What are you talking about? What choice?

TEACHER: When are you going to get up?

SUSIE: I don't know . . . maybe never. (Falls back on pillow)

TEACHER: OK, let's see if we can help Susie. First, let's help her think about all her options. (Invite kids to suggest to Susie what her options are. Possibilities may include: getting up now, sleeping 5 more minutes, staying in bed all day, ignoring her mom and getting up whenever she feels like it, etc.)

SUSIE: Gosh, I didn't know getting up in the morning was such a major task! Now I'm all confused. What should I do?

TEACHER: Last week we learned that all our choices have consequences, and we need to think about the consequences of our choices ahead of time. Now that we've thought about all your options, perhaps we can eliminate some of them by thinking about the consequences they may have. But first, let's add one more thing to think about. Not only can we think about the consequences of our choices, but we can think about what God's Word teaches us, too. Susie, can you think of anything in God's Word that can help you make a good choice right now?

SUSIE: Well, it says we need to obey our parents. And . . . let's see, I think Proverbs says something about not being lazy. And . . . well, there isn't a verse that says so, but I guess God wouldn't be too happy if I threw my alarm clock through the window or anything like that.

TEACHER: That's good thinking! Now, can you think of other things that can help you make this choice?

SUSIE: Well, even though it would feel good to sleep another couple hours, I really don't want to be late for school. I'd hate to have everyone look at me when I came in late. Besides, I don't think my mom would give me an excuse note for sleeping in 'cause I stayed up to watch a movie.

TEACHER: OK! So, after thinking about it, which choice seems best for you right now?

SUSIE: Groan! I'm not sure I like it, but getting up does seem to be the best choice. (She gets up and rolls up her sleeping bag. As she walks off, she calls out . . .) I'm coming, Mom! I *am up!* I'll be right down for breakfast!

Following the skit, gather your class together again around the table, or continue to sit in a circle on the floor. **Do you think Susie made the best choice? Why or why not? Give your kids a chance to respond. They may have been in a situation similar to Susie! Why is it important to stop and think about all our possible alternatives before making decisions?** (It gives us time to think of possibilities we might not think of right away; it keeps us from making mistakes by acting too quickly.)

Now spend a few minutes identifying options for real situations your students are facing in their lives. **Let's see if we can practice finding options for some choices you have to make, or your friends have to make. Would anyone like to share a decision that kids your age have to make, and let us as a class find some options for it?** Give students time to respond. When a situation is suggested, ask the class to brainstorm all possible options. Remind the kids to think creatively and to keep thinking long enough to come up with as many choices as possible. I hope you are beginning to see that whatever the choice, you have many possible options!

Refer to the Unit Affirmation poster. Have kids read together the affirmation, I CAN THINK BEFORE I CHOOSE! **Last week we said that we need to think ahead about what the consequences of our choices will be. Today, let's add to our poster. What else can we think about before we choose?** Let kids respond. Then, write these two phrases: "Options," and "God's Word."

We have talked a lot about thinking of our options. Now let's spend some time seeing how thinking about God's Word can help us make wise decisions!

Searching the Scriptures (20 minutes)

Display the ordinary cup, decorative cup, large cup, and measuring cup for all the students to see. **Which cup do you think is the most important one? Why?** Your students will probably pick either the decorative or largest cup. **The most important cup in this group is the measuring cup. Can you tell me why that's true?** Let your students give their answers. Help them see that this cup provides an unchanging standard. It settles all arguments because its measurements or rules never change. It remains the same and so can always be trusted. Because of all these reasons it is the most important cup of all. **How is this measuring cup like the Bible?** Point out that the wisdom God's Word gives can be trusted in all situations because like God, who is all-knowing and all-wise, it never changes. It can be used to see if our choices or actions measure up to God's will. We can trust it to be an unchanging guide which will help us make wise choices.

Divide your class into small groups of not more than three or four people.

Provide half these groups with toothpicks or some kind of game cards. Give the other groups a number of children's building blocks such as Legos. Ask each team to build a house with their materials. The team that builds the biggest, most secure house will win the title of "Master Builders." Give them a few minutes to work on this, then call time. Judge the structures and praise the winners.

How easy was it to build with your materials? (The ones who had cards found it more difficult than those with the blocks.) **How did you feel about having to compete with teams that had stronger materials to work with?** They will probably feel the competition was unfair. **Trying to make choices on our own is a bit like building with toothpicks or cards. It's a shaky business that is liable to end in disaster.**

Have students turn to Matthew 7:24-27. Ask a volunteer to read these verses. **Jesus says both these builders heard His words. What was the difference between them?** (The wise one put His words into practice while the foolish one didn't.) **Knowing what the Bible says isn't enough. We must also do what it says.**

Have your students look up II Timothy 3:16, 17. Ask someone to read these verses. **Who is the real author of the Bible?** (God.) **How is His book to be used?** (To teach us how to live right, correct faults, give us wise advice) **What will you be able to do when you put God's Word into practice?** Help your students see that when they apply what they hear or read, they will be ready to serve God and have all the wisdom they need to make wise choices. To help people avoid making mistakes the Bible gives them a preview of what happens when they make a foolish choice. Instead of having to learn things the hard way by our own experiences and mistakes, God's Word provides a warning system which points out consequences caused by foolish choices.

We've already seen the consequences of a foolish choice in the story of the two builders. Can you think of other Bible stories that illustrate foolish choices? (Adam and Eve eating from the forbidden tree; Esau choosing a bowl of stew over his spiritual inheritance; Haman trying to kill Mordecai and God's people; Ananias and Sapphira lying to Peter about the sale of their property; etc.) **Why did God tell us both the good and bad things about Bible people?** (So we could learn from their mistakes and avoid making the same kind of foolish choices.)

Our Unit Verse talks about the importance of following God's Word. Have the class read or recite the verse together. "The fear of the Lord is the beginning of wisdom; all who follow his precepts have good understanding" Psalm 111:10. **God is all-knowing, all-seeing, all-wise. When we base our choices on what He says, we have God's power to help us. That added power is what enables us to make wise decisions. However, there is an invisible *IF* in this verse. We must not only know what God's Word says, but we**

must also do what it says. Point out that knowing God's Word says we shouldn't steal is of no value to us if we choose to steal a candy bar. That kind of senseless choice ends up in a disaster like the foolish man building his house on the sand.

Have kids reflect on what they've learned about heeding God's Word and add comments to the graffiti wall. Some examples might be: Save heartache–do what the Bible says; Ignore the Bible now–pay for it later; God's wisdom–it's the real thing; God's Word—You're gonna love what it does for you.

✔ **Living the Lesson** (5-10 minutes)

Distribute "Look It Up" activity sheet (page 60). Have one group of students work on the first situation, another group of kids work on the second situation, and a third group of kids work on the third situation.

What do you think Corey should do? Why? (Most kids will agree that he should clean up his room instead of going to play ball. If he doesn't he will disappoint his mom; get in trouble with her; might get grounded for breaking his promise; lose the privilege of being on the team.) **What are some options that Corey could use?** (He could clean up as much as possible before practice. Then he could talk it over with his mom and offer to clean up the rest of the room later on in the day.) **What might his mom think of this solution?** (She might think it was wise of him to discuss it with her rather than just ran out on his promise; think he could be trusted to keep his word; be more willing to give him other options in the future.)

What are some things that could happen if Jill starts a rumor about Lynn? (She might cause the class to have to choose between believing her or Lynn; the teacher might get angry and discipline her; Lynn would just start some other rumor and pretty soon the girls would be constant enemies.) **Would getting even with Lynn really help Jill?** (No, it would only prolong the conflict between them and in the long run Jill would become a bitter, angry person.) **What might happen if Jill obeys God's Word and forgives Lynn?** (Lynn might feel sorry and tell the kids she lied; she might become Jill's friend; Jill would have an opportunity to talk to Lynn about Jesus.)

What do you think Kevin should do? (Most kids would agree that he should go in person.) **What good things would his visit do?** (Make the visit a family outing; mean more to Grandma than if he just sends his love and greeting; please God by his obedience; show Jesus he loves Him.)

Close with prayer thanking God for giving us the Bible to help us make wise choices.

How Many Choices Can I Find? ✔

#1: No school today! How many things can you think of to do?

_____

_____

_____

_____

_____

_____

_____

_____

_____

_____

_____

_____

_____

_____

_____

_____

_____

_____

_____

_____

_____

#2: It's your birthday, and Grandma gave you $5! How many ways can you think of to spend it?

_____

_____

_____

_____

_____

_____

_____

_____

_____

_____

_____

_____

_____

_____

_____

_____

_____

_____

_____

_____

_____

Read each story. Look up the references and check out what God's Word says. Make your choices and write them on the lines.

Corey has been so busy with school and ball practice that his room has become a disaster area. He promised his mom he would clean it this Saturday.

Matt called right after breakfast on Saturday to say that a few of the team thought they needed some extra practice and were getting together in an hour. Corey groaned. He knew he could use the extra help but he could never get everything picked up by then. What should he do?

Look up: Matthew 5:37a; Philippians 2:14; Colossians 3:20

Jill was elected class president last week. She was thrilled but her happiness soon turned into frustration. Lynn told everyone that Jill only won because her mom and the teacher, Mrs. Grant, are such good friends. She said Mrs. Grant changed the vote count so Jill would win. Jill knows that she won fairly and Lynn is only being mean because she lost. She feels like starting a rumor about Lynn to get even. What should Jill do?

Look up: Proverbs 26:18-20; Ephesians 4:31, 32

Kevin's grandmother lives in a nursing home. His parents are going to see her this afternoon. They want Kevin to go with them, but have left the choice up to him. He loves his grandma and knows he should go along, but he dislikes the smells in the building. Besides, Grandma is getting so forgetful that she keeps repeating the same things so it gets boring to try to hold a conversation. Maybe he could just send his love and a greeting. What should he do?

Look up: Matthew 25:37-40; Hebrews 13:16

Lesson 3

Who You Gonna Call?

Aim: That your students will identify wise people who can help them make decisions and call upon them when needed.

Scripture: Exodus 18:13-26

Unit Verse: The fear of the Lord is the beginning of wisdom; all who follow his precepts have good understanding. Psalm 111:10

Unit Affirmation: I CAN THINK BEFORE I CHOOSE!

 **Planning Ahead**

1. Write 20 Bible trivia questions if needed (See SETTING THE STAGE)
2. Cut a strip of tracing or tissue paper 1 1/2" x 11"
3. Photocopy activity sheets (pages 67 and 68)–one for each student
4. On 3" x 5" cards write out the three situations found in LIVING THE LESSON section

1 Setting the Stage (5-10 minutes)

WHAT YOU'LL DO

- Play a cooperation game to emphasize that sometimes we need to ask others for help

WHAT YOU'LL NEED

- A Bible Trivia, Jr. Trivia, or other question/answer type game

2 Introducing the Issue (20 minutes)

WHAT YOU'LL DO

- Identify the signs that let us know when we need to ask for help
- Use an activity sheet to make a personal list of people who can help when needed
- Add a phrase to the Unit Affirmation Poster

WHAT YOU'LL NEED

- A sheet of poster board and a set of markers (or, an overhead transparency and projector)
- "Help Hotline" Activity Sheet (page 67)
- Unit Affirmation Poster

3 Searching the Scriptures (20 minutes)

WHAT YOU'LL DO

- See an object lesson to note how wise people can help us make choices
- Observe how a wise relative helped a leader solve a problem

WHAT YOU'LL NEED

- Strip of tracing or tissue paper 1 1/2" x 11"
- Flashlight
- Bibles
- "Choicebusters" Activity Sheet (page 68)

4 Living the Lesson (5-10 minutes)

WHAT YOU'LL DO

- Rehearse asking others for help

WHAT YOU'LL NEED

- 3 roleplaying situations on index cards

 *Lesson 3*

 Setting the Stage (5-10 minutes)

As students arrive today, involve them in a game which will allow them to ask for help when they need it. You will need to bring a Bible Trivia, Junior Trivia, or other question and answer type game. If you do not have access to a game, you can make up 20 or so of your own Bible trivia questions.

Begin as soon as you have four students. Set up two teams and add to them as students come into class. **To play the game today, I am going to ask a question to the first person on the first team. Give an answer if you know it. If you don't know the answer, ask your team for help. I'll continue asking questions from team to team. But remember, you can always ask your team members for help.** Award points for correct responses. Continue play until all students have arrived and had a chance to play for a few minutes.

 Introducing the Issue (20 minutes)

Explain that today the class is going to talk about a very important part of good decision making: Asking for Help! **We just played a game during which we sometimes needed to ask our teammates for help. Although that was just a game, it reminds us of a very important life skill; everyone needs to ask for help sometimes! In fact, God has designed us so we would need to ask each other for help. It is *good* to need help sometimes. The important thing is to know *when* to ask for help, and *who* to ask.**

Display a piece of poster board where all can see it clearly, and so that you can write on it. As you begin, draw a large stick figure in the center of it.

> **OPTIONAL:** If you are artistic, or want to spend more time on this, you could prepare this poster ahead of time, drawing a nicely done, complete picture of a child.

It's easy for us to think we have to make all decisions on our own, and not "bother" anyone with our problems. However, there are some signs that can tell us when we need to ask for help. Many of those signs are in our bodies. Learning to pay attention to what our bodies tell us is an important part of knowing when we need to ask for help. What are some of those signs? Let kids respond. As ideas are shared, draw a line from the part of the body that is affected and write the symptom on the poster.

Possibilities include:

HEAD – Get headaches; feel confused; don't understand something

EYES – Cry a lot; can't sleep; saw something you can't forget

MOUTH – Can't eat or you eat too much

HEART – Feel very sad; something gives you a "broken" heart

STOMACH – Tight knots from feeling angry or anxious

KNEES – Fear causes your knees to knock

FEET – Run away from certain people or problems

When the poster is complete, summarize the discussion. **These are all important signs that we need to pay attention to. They all say the same thing:** *it's ti'me to ask for help!* **But the next question is,** *who can I ask for help when I need it?*

Distribute "Help Hotline" activity sheet (page 67). Tell students they will be making a list of people in their lives they can turn to during those times when they need help making decisions. **Before you begin to make your lists, what are some of the characteristics of the people you'd like to ask for help when you need it?** (They can be trusted; they are both good listeners and wise; they have information you may need to make a good decision; they are good huggers–sometimes we just need to be held for a few moments.)

Now, think carefully about these characteristics. Who do you know that can be trusted to turn to when you need help? Give the kids some time to think about individuals and write their names on their "Help Hotline" sheet.

Encourage them to take these home, discuss them with a parent, and add phone numbers. Then they can put the lists somewhere in their rooms where they can get to it easily whenever they need to ask someone for help.

Display the Unit Affirmation Poster. Have the class say the Unit Affirmation together: I CAN THINK BEFORE I CHOOSE! Review the phrases that were added the past two weeks, and ask for volunteers to share what each one means. **What did we talk about today that is something we can think about before we choose?** Let kids respond, and then add the phrase, *who can help.* Remember, making wise choices is important! You don't have to make hasty decisions. YOU CAN THINK BEFORE YOU CHOOSE!

Everyone needs to ask for help now and then. The Bible tells us about an adult that needed help with a problem.

 # Searching the Scriptures (20 minutes)

Use this object lesson to show your students how wise people can shed light

on their problems and give them the direction they need. **When we have a tough problem facing us and we need to make a choice, it can seem to tie us up in "knots."**

Fold the 1 1/2" x 11" tissue paper in half, lengthwise so it now measures 3/4" x 11". Tie a flat knot near the left-hand end of the strip by folding the left end over the right one and pulling it through to the left again. Be sure to keep this knot flat. Fold the right-

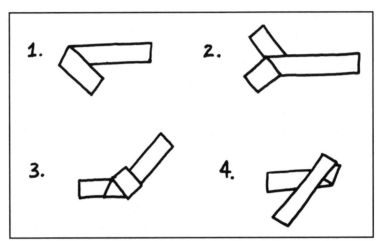

hand side of the strip over this knot, keeping its top edge even with the top edge of the knot. This right-hand end is now pointing downward. **We try to think the problem through to see the possible consequences of various choices but are still baffled. Sometimes we worry and wonder if there is any solution. That's when we need to seek the advice of wise people who can help us make good decisions.**

When we let their guidance shine light on the problem (shine flashlight through the knot) **then we can see beyond the knot to something more.**

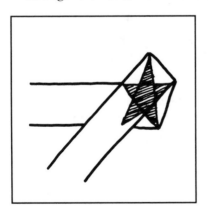

What do you see? (A five-pointed star.) **Just as the Star of Hope guided the wise men when Jesus was born, wise, godly people can shed light on our problems and give us the direction we need.**

Have students turn to Exodus 18:13-26. Ask volunteers to read the verses. **What was Moses' problem?** (Too many people were coming to him for advice. He needed help.) **What help did Jethro give to Moses?** (He suggested breaking up the responsibility for judging the people so Moses wouldn't wear himself out.)

Hand out copies of "Choicebusters" activity sheet (page 68). This skit will help your kids see how wise people can help them make decisions. You will need three people to read the parts. Everyone joins in the theme rap which introduces and closes the play.

Optional: This is a fun skit to perform. If you have time and a room that permits, let your kids enjoy this by acting it out.

Today we are going to visit Choicebusters' Central. It is the headquarters for a group of capable people known as Choicebusters. These keen investigators are known for their wisdom and insight. They are experienced in helping people make good choices. Let's see what's going on there today.

Read through the skit, and when you have finished, talk about it. **How do you think Moses felt about his problem before finding someone to help him?** (Depressed; unable to do anything about it; worried.) **How do you think he felt about asking for help?** (Probably hesitant; scared; didn't know who to go to or what to ask for.)

How do you think Jethro felt about giving Moses advice? (Happy to help out; eager to help him; wanted the best for him and the people.) Emphasize that Jethro loved Moses and really wanted to help him. He was neither judgmental nor accusing in his advice. His only concern was to relieve Moses' burden and help him function more efficiently.

Many kids are hesitant to ask for advice from people because they fear they will be scolded or ridiculed. Real-life choicebusters help determine the underlying problem; are not afraid of it; help others; make plans first, then act to solve problems; know that by solving one problem you can go on to others. When kids know they will be listened to and lovingly helped, they are more willing to approach counselors.

Have the class read or recite the Unit Verse together. "The fear of the Lord is the beginning of wisdom; all who follow his precepts have good understanding." Psalm 111:10. **According to this verse, who are the people who have good understanding?** (People who follow God's laws; people who fear [respect] the Lord.) **When you have identified these people then you can ask them to help you make decisions. They have more experience and resources than you do.** Point out to your students that knowledge is not the same as wisdom. There are a lot of intelligent people who don't respect God or do what His Word says. They may appear to be smart but in reality they are as foolish as the man who built his house on the sand if their intelligence is based only on human knowledge.

Have students add comments about calling upon wise people to the graffiti wall. Examples are: Being with wise people rubs off; Get wise advice—it never fails; Reach out and touch someone-ask for help; Call Choicebusters—they care.

Lesson 3

✔ Living the Lesson (5-10 minutes)

Gather the class together to roleplay some situations when they may need to ask for help. **Who are some people you can go to when you need a Choicebuster–someone to help?** (Parent; friend's parent; teacher; policeman; Sunday school teacher; coach; school principal; school counselor; nurse; neighbor; social worker.) List these possibilities on the chalkboard.

Use roleplay to allow your kids to practice how they would ask a wise person for advice. Distribute the three index cards with the following situations written on them to three students. Have them read aloud the situations. After each problem is read have the class match a Choicebuster to it. In some cases there can be more than one Choicebuster that would match the problem but for the sake of simplifying the roleplay, select only one for that part of this activity. Ask volunteers to take the roles of the person making the choice and the Choicebuster.

After the roleplay ask some discussion questions. The first questions should deal with the roleplay itself. **How do you think the characters in this situation were feeling? Why did they act or react that way? If the kid needed to ask someone for advice again, what could s/he do better or differently?** The second set of questions helps students personally apply what they learned by the roleplay. **What makes kids or Choicebusters feel, act, or react the way they do? If you were going to ask another Choicebuster for advice what would you do differently?** If you have a longer class period you could repeat the roleplays using different kids to play the parts and choosing different Choicebusters.

Situation #1-You know Keri is taking drugs. You think you should tell somebody so they can help her, but she says she won't be your friend if you do.

Situation #2-You struck out and the team lost the game. When you were walking home, Scott was waiting and hit you. "That's for losing," he shouted. You like playing ball, but are afraid to play again.

Situation #3-Char has trouble with math and has been pestering you to let her copy your papers. You finally let her copy your paper and the teacher caught both of you. Char told the teacher you were the one who copied her paper and the teacher believed her.

Have kids think of a wise person who has helped them in the past and silently thank God for him/her or pray for courage to go to a Choicebuster for advice. Close with a praise prayer to God for wise people who care about others and are willing to help them make good choices.

Help Hotline ✓

Everyone Needs Help Sometimes!
WHEN I NEED HELP, I CAN ASK:

Other Relatives:

_____

Phone # _____

_____

Phone # _____

_____

Phone # _____

People at My Church:

_____

Phone # _____

_____

Phone # _____

Family Members:

_____

Phone # _____

_____

Phone # _____

_____

Phone # _____

People at My School:

_____

Phone # _____

_____

Phone # _____

_____

Phone # _____

Others:

_____

Phone # _____

_____

Phone # _____

_____

Phone # _____

The Best HUGGER I Know is:
Pets, Stuffed Animals, etc.

_____

I Can "Talk" to:
Pets, Stuffed Animals, etc.

_____

Scene: Choicebusters Central. (The secretary is at her desk. Moses enters, setting off the customer alert button and theme.)

All: WHO YOU GONNA CALL when you don't know what to do? WHO YOU GONNA CALL when a choice is buggin' you? CHOICEBUSTERS, yeah, yeah–THAT'S WHO!

Secretary: Welcome to Choicebusters' Central. Our sensational staff dazzlingly determines puzzling problems, faces facts and happily helps others. Now, what can we do for you today, Mr. . . ..?

Moses: Moses. I'm not sure how to begin.

Secretary: The best way is to start at the beginning. Suppose you rate the problem from 1-10 with 10 being the hardest. In your opinion, Mr. Moses, how would you rate this problem?

Moses: Just call me Moses. I think this is a Class 10 problem.

Secretary: I see, then I suggest you see Choicebuster Jethro. His office is down the hall, first door to the right.

Moses (walks around and knocks at door): Jethro, that's the same name as my father-in-law. Could it be? (shakes head) Naw!

Jethro: Come in. Well, if it isn't Moses! You look tired. Sit down and tell me all about it, Son.

Moses (looks surprised, sits down): Dad! I didn't know you were a Choicebuster.

Jethro: A little part-time job to keep me active. I've been watching you. Right away I could see you had a

problem with all those people standing around you every day from morning until night! Tell me, why do you settle all those arguments yourself? Are you some kind of workaholic or do you get paid extra for overtime? Zipporah and the boys miss you. So do I.

Moses (shoulders sagging): Well, the people come to me to get God's help in solving disagreements. I tell them who's right based on God's laws and teachings. I know they need help, but frankly I need time off. I kept hoping that after we crossed the Red Sea I could take a vacation, but things only got worse.

Jethro: No wonder! You're not Superman, you know. And the people are complaining as much as you are. It's important that you talk to God for the people and of course they need to be taught God's laws, but I've got a plan that can help everybody.

Moses (sits up, looking interested): I'm listening!

Jethro: Why not choose some executive-type people you can trust. You know the kind—respect God, refuse bribes. Put them in charge of smaller groups and let them settle the minor squabbles. Then, when the biggies come up, they can send them to you. How does that sound?

Moses: Sounds good. I'll ask God what He says. If I get the go–ahead we'll put it into effect right away. Why didn't I think of that?

Jethro: Maybe because you're not an experienced Choicebuster yet.

Moses (smiles and shakes hands with Jethro): Thanks, Dad. I'm sure glad you wanted to help. You Choicebusters are terrific!

Jethro: You're welcome, Son. That's what we're here for. I'll tell Zipporah and the boys you'll be home early tonight.

All: WHO YOU GONNA CALL when you don't know what to do? WHO YOU GONNA' CALL when a choice is buggin' you? CHOICEBUSTERS, yeah,
 yeah–THAT'S WHO!

I Challenge You!

Aim: That your students will wisely choose to follow God's way.

Scripture: Esther 4:1-16, 7:1-4, 8:7, 8, 16, 17

Unit Verse: The fear of the Lord is the beginning of wisdom; all who follow his precepts have good understanding. Psalm 111:10

Unit Affirmation: I CAN THINK BEFORE I CHOOSE!

 Planning Ahead

1. Set up three activity centers as described in SETTING THE STAGE.
2. Prepare Bible charades. (See INTRODUCING THE ISSUE.)
3. Photocopy activity sheets (pages 75 and 76)–one for each student.

1 Setting the Stage (5-10 minutes)

WHAT YOU'LL DO

- Participate in several activity centers to discover how the Holy Spirit helps us make wise choices

WHAT YOU'LL NEED

- Toaster, tape player, telephone
- Bread

2 Introducing the Issue

WHAT YOU'LL DO

- Play Bible charades and discuss examples of people who chose God's way, and some who did not
- Make a list of characteristics of people who choose to follow God
- Review the Unit Affirmation poster

WHAT YOU'LL NEED

- 3" x 5" cards prepared with the assignments for Bible charades
- "Choosing God's Way" Activity Sheet (page 75)
- Unit Affirmation Poster

3 Searching the Scriptures (20 minutes)

WHAT YOU'LL DO

- Solve a puzzle to consider how God honors those who choose to follow Him
- Play a game to see how students need God's wisdom in their lives
- Make stickers as reminders to make wise choices

WHAT YOU'LL NEED

- Bibles
- "A-Maz-In' Esther," Activity Sheet (page 76)
- Blank sticker badges

4 Living the Lesson (5-10 minutes)

WHAT YOU'LL DO

- Provide an opportunity to choose God's way

WHAT YOU'LL NEED

- Several large items such as cardboard box, cushion, chair

Lesson 4

✓ Setting the Stage (5-10 minutes)

Before students arrive, set up three centers around the room. Each center will involve the kids in a small task (no longer than 2 minutes to complete), using an object that needs to be connected to a power source (electricity or batteries) to work.

At the first center have a tape player with a headset. Students will listen to a tape of children's music or something similar for a minute or two.

At the second center have a toaster. Allow students to make pieces of toast, sharing one piece between two kids.

Finally, at the third center have a telephone. List the phone number for the local time, and ask kids to call. They can check the time on their watches or the room clock. You probably will not have a phone jack in your room. In that case, leave the phone unconnected, and let kids reflect on their inability to complete this task, due to the *lack* of a power source.

As students arrive, allow them to circulate among the centers and complete the tasks at each one. When all have arrived and had a few minutes to see the centers, call time and gather everyone together.

✓ Introducing the Issue (20 minutes)

For the past few minutes, you have been doing some things at the tables around the room. Now, here's a riddle for you to solve. What do all the items you used at each table have in common? Divide the kids into pairs, and give them two minutes to come up with an answer. At the end of the 2 minutes, call time and discuss their answers.

The answer to our riddle is that each of the items you used today needs a power source to work. Without electricity, batteries, a phone jack, etc., many of the things we use every day won't work. As Christians, we have a power source, too. What is our power source? (The Holy Spirit living in us.) **What does having the Holy Spirit within us have to do with making wise choices?** (When we ask for His help, the Spirit helps us know what God would want us to do. See John 14:26.)

Today we are going to talk about what it means to "Choose

God's Way." The first thing we need to know is that the best choices we can make are ones that follow God's plan for us, and God's Spirit is the best source of help we can have to make those choices. We can ask Him for help anytime, and He will guide our thinking in the right direction. Now let's take a look at some Bible people who had to make some choices, and see what else we can discover about choosing God's way.

Divide the kids into four groups. Give each group a 3" x 5" card on which you have copied the following information (one Bible story per card). Instruct them that they are to work out a simple skit depicting their assigned Bible story.

Group #1: Noah and the Ark – Genesis 6:11–14, 17–19, 22

Group #2: Abraham and Sarah in Egypt – Genesis 12:10–20

Group #3: Jonah and the Fish – Jonah 1

Group #4: Jesus Is Tempted – Matthew 4:1–11

Give the groups 5-7 minutes to complete their assignments. When the time is up, gather everyone together again, and distribute activity sheet, "Choosing God's Way" (page 75). **Now that you've had some time to prepare, we'll give each group a few minutes to act out their story while the rest of us try to guess the Bible story.** When the story has been guessed, lead a discussion using the questions on the activity sheet.

When you are discussing Noah, help the kids understand that building the ark was not an easy thing to do. Noah did *not* live near water! Deciding to follow God's directions probably meant that he was ridiculed by everyone in his community.

When you are discussing Abraham, point out that he makes an unwise choice. He was afraid, and chose to tell a lie rather than trusting God. His lie gets him into trouble, and he learns that trusting God is a wiser choice than lying!

When discussing Jonah, help the kids see that because of his unwise choice, Jonah discovers rather dramatically that choosing God's way is wiser than going our own!

As you discuss Jesus, mention that He showed us how to use Scripture as a means for making wise choices. He chooses to obey God's Word, rather than follow Satan's way.

When all four skits have been presented, work together as a class to fill in the bottom portion of the activity sheet. **What are some characteristics of people who choose to follow God's way?** (Have the

Holy Spirit inside to help; obey God's Word; stand up for what they believe, even if others don't understand or make fun of them.)

Refer to the Unit Affirmation poster as a way to summarize what it means to choose God's way. Read the affirmation and all the phrases together. **These words tell us what it means to choose God's way. Now, let's look more closely at one person in the Bible who trusted God to help her make a really important decision!**

 # Searching the Scriptures (20 minutes)

Briefly explain the background of this story before reading it in the Bible. The Jewish orphan girl Esther became the Persian queen when she was chosen by the king from many other beautiful candidates. Her uncle Mordecai apparently served at the king's palace and counseled her not to tell anyone she was Jewish. Haman was a powerful friend of the king and enemy of Mordecai and the Jews. He talked the king into believing the Jews were Persia's enemies and setting a date when they would all be killed. Have kids turn to Esther 4:1-16 and take turns reading it.

Esther really had an important decision to make. It would not only affect her own life but that of the lives of all the Jews in Persia. Point out that Esther took the same steps your kids have been learning to follow when making a choice. She asked her Choicebuster, Mordecai, for advice and also sought out God's wisdom through prayer. Explain that in her day, there was little Scripture to read, but she prayed and meditated on God for three days before making a decision. Now she was ready to think through, step by step, the consequences her decision might bring.

Hand out copies of "A-Maz-In' Esther" activity sheet (page 76). It will let your kids see both the long- and short-range possibilities of her choice. Allow time for students to work through the maze individually.

Ask kids to turn to Esther 7:1-4 and 8:7, 8, 16, 17 and take turns reading it. **Did Esther know when she made that first choice what honors God would give her?** (No.) **Then why do you think she chose to follow God when the risk was so great?** (Because she loved Him, knew it was the right thing to do, knew her people were depending on her.) Help your students understand that they should follow God because they love Him and want to obey Him, not because of rewards. God deserves our worship and honor because of who He is, not what He gives us.

How do you think Esther felt when she went into the inner court to talk to the king? (Frightened; nervous; confident that she was doing the right thing.) Help your kids realize that even though they make the right choices it is not uncommon or wrong to have conflicting emotions. Esther was convinced God wanted her to do this thing, but she had no written assurance that things would turn out as wonderfully as they did. We are fortunate that we can read about her example and that of other wise people who decided to follow God. In every case we will find that God honors those who choose to follow Him. The immediate consequences may be frightening and not look like God's blessing, but if we remain faithful the end results are worth all the struggles.

Be careful not to mislead your students by promising them a struggle-free life of ease if they choose to follow God. Jesus told us that in order to follow Him fully, we must deny ourselves and take up our cross daily. Not all rewards may be material or even come during our lifetime, but they are definitely worth all the in-between struggles. We will have problems as long as we are in this world, but when we follow God, we no longer face them alone. God is with us and we can call upon all His resources.

What were some of the blessings God gave Esther for following Him? (Haman's property; the privilege of writing another law allowing the Jews to defend themselves; her life; the lives of all the Jews; seeing other nationalities turn to worship God.) Although they aren't included in these Scripture passages, other benefits included elevating her uncle Mordecai to the position of second in command of all Persia and the executions of Haman and his ten sons as well as thousands of the Jews enemies. The Jewish holiday of Purim was begun and continues to be celebrated annually by Jews down to the present time.

What might have been some of the consequences if Esther had chosen differently? (She might have been killed; all the Jews would have been murdered; she would have lived a life of fear and lies; evil and false gods could have taken the place of God.) Help your students understand that the choices they make not only affect them personally but also influence people around them.

Review the Unit Verse, Psalm 111:10. "The fear of the Lord is the beginning of wisdom; all who follow his precepts have good understanding." Finish the graffiti wall by adding comments on God's rewards for those who follow Him. Examples might be: Serve God—the

benefits are out of this world; Choose God—it pays. Pass out the sticker badges. Kids can make stickers to take home using a favorite graffiti statement from the wall or by creating a new one.

 # Living the Lesson (5-10 minutes)

Play a game for application time. Have your students stand shoulder to shoulder on one side of the room and blindfold them. Place several large items such as a cardboard box, big cushion, and a chair, as obstructions in the middle of room. If your classroom is small and you can't move the furniture, use your table and chairs to form the obstacles by rearranging them. You may also want to darken the room. The kids must find their way across the room without help and form a line on the opposite side. **What you just did shows what it's like to make your choices or live without God. You hope you're headed in the right direction and won't bump into too many problems. You find the obstacles are bigger than you thought and you can end up with bumps and bruises.**

Remove the blindfolds. Turn on lights if they were off. Now have kids cross to the other side and form a line. **That was much easier, wasn't it? That what it's like when you follow God's way. The obstacles are there, but you have the power to see them and cross safely.** Have the kids help you move the obstacles to one side.

Give your students an opportunity to choose to follow God. Ask kids to line up again on the opposite side of the room to you. I'm going to give each of you an opportunity to choose to follow God. Bow your heads and pray silently. **Those of you who choose to follow God's way may cross over to me.** Close in prayer.

Choosing God's Way

#1: Bible Person_____
The choice this person made was: WISE or UNWISE
The consequences (good and bad) of this choice were:

_____

_____

_____

#2: Bible Person_____
The choice this person made was: WISE or UNWISE
The consequences (good and bad) of this choice were:

_____

_____

_____

#3: Bible Person_____
The choice this person made was: WISE or UNWISE
The consequences (good and bad) of this choice were:

_____

_____

_____

#4: Bible Person_____
The choice this person made was: WISE or UNWISE
The consequences (good and bad) of this choice were:

_____

_____

_____

A PERSON WHO CHOOSES GOD'S WAY...

1._____

2._____

3._____

☑ A-MAZ-IN' Esther

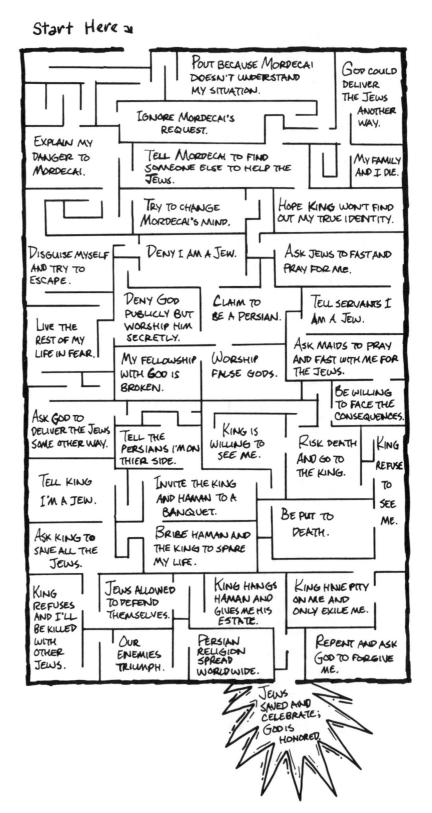

Start Here ➔

Pout because Mordecai doesn't understand my situation.

God could deliver the Jews another way.

Ignore Mordecai's request.

Explain my danger to Mordecai.

Tell Mordecai to find someone else to help the Jews.

My family and I die.

Try to change Mordecai's mind.

Hope King won't find out my true identity.

Disguise myself and try to escape.

Deny I am a Jew.

Ask Jews to fast and pray for me.

Deny God publicly but worship him secretly.

Claim to be a Persian.

Tell servants I am a Jew.

Live the rest of my life in fear.

My fellowship with God is broken.

Worship false gods.

Ask maids to pray and fast with me for the Jews.

Be willing to face the consequences.

Ask God to deliver the Jews some other way.

Tell the Persians I'm on thier side.

King is willing to see me.

Risk death and go to the King.

King refuse to see me.

Tell king I'm a Jew.

Invite the king and Haman to a banquet.

Be put to death.

Ask king to save all the Jews.

Bribe Haman and the king to spare my life.

King refuses and I'll be killed with other Jews.

Jews allowed to defend themselves.

King hangs Haman and gives me his estate.

King have pity on me and only exile me.

Our enemies triumph.

Persian religion spread worldwide.

Repent and ask God to forgive me.

Jews saved and celebrate; God is honored.

I, Queen Esther, have a big problem. The lives of all the Jews in Persia depend on my decision. Please help me through this maze and solve the problem. "Could-bes" resulting from my choices are:

Service Projects for Making Choices

✓ 1. During this unit, ask kids to bring 50¢ each week for a special service project. Then, on the last week, using the principles they have learned in this unit, involve your group in making a choice as to how to spend the money. For example, have them list all the options they can think of for the project. If they can't think of any, ask who could be consulted to help find a project. Don't forget to ask for the Holy Spirit's guidance and to think about what God's Word says. When several choices have been identified, agree on one and make the necessary arrangements to use the money appropriately. Possible projects: a special missionary need, a local food or clothing shelter, needed toys for your own preschool classrooms, etc.

✓ 2. Your class can help younger kids learn how to make wise decisions by putting on the plays, "The Fascinating Case of the Five Failing Flames," and "Choicebusters." If desired, these skits could be adapted for puppet plays.

You might also decide to do some of the roleplays to illustrate the differences between wise and foolish choices or how to go about making wise choices.

Finding and Keeping Friends

Friendships can bring us all the best things in life, but they can also be a source of great pain. Although God has designed us to need relationships with others, it takes skill and wisdom to find, develop, and keep healthy friendships. As Juniors, your kids are just beginning to understand how important friendships are in their lives. They are discovering that belonging to the group is all important, as is looking, talking, and acting "right." It is also an age of experimentation, and you will find many of them awkward at relating to friends in positive ways.

Oftentimes, kids are left to learn about friendships from their own feelings and what they see modeled around them by parents, other adults, TV, etc. In this unit, however, you will have the opportunity to guide your students to learn biblical principles and basic skills of being a good friend. Through the Unit Verse and the Unit Affirmation, your kids will discover that Jesus' relationship to us is our standard of what it means to be a good friend to others.

Helping your students discover that Jesus is the best friend they can have, and how to follow His example of being a friend to others, will equip them to enjoy healthy relationships now and in the future.

✓ Friendship Overview

Unit Verse: My command is this: Love each other as I have loved you. John 15:12

Unit Affirmation: I CAN BE A FRIEND TO OTHERS AS JESUS IS A FRIEND TO ME!

LESSON	TITLE	OBJECTIVE	SCRIPTURE BASE
Lesson #1	What Makes a Good Friend?	That your students will be a good friend to others.	I Samuel 18:1-4
Lesson #2	You Don't Belong!	That your students will abandon cliques and pattern their friendships after God's all-inclusive love.	Luke 10:25-37
Lesson #3	Get Off My Case!	That your students will stop criticizing and saying put-downs to each other but, instead, support each other.	Numbers 12:1-15
Lesson #4	Will You Still Be My Friend?	That your students will understand that no matter what changes they experience in their friendships they can have Jesus as their unchanging, forever friend.	John 15:12-17
Lesson #5	Can You Keep a Secret?	That your students will understand that God wants us to be trustworthy and not betray a friend's confidence.	I Samuel 20:5-42

Partners

For the next few weeks your junior-age child will be part of a group learning about Friendship. Partners is a planned parent piece to keep you informed of what will be taught during this exciting series.

PREVIEW...

Learning About Friendships

Everyone needs friends. In fact, God designed us to need others; none of us was created to "go it alone" through life. Friendships can bring us the very best life has to offer, but, they can also be a source of much frustration and pain. It takes skill and wisdom to find, nurture, and keep good friends! Your children are now at the age where friendships are important, but they have not yet learned the skills needed to relate to others in satisfying ways. In the next few years, they will be experimenting with various relational styles based on how they see parents, other adults, and peers interacting with others. That's why now is an important time for you to offer them clear guidance on what it means to be a good friend to others. In the next few weeks, your kids will be exploring various aspects of friendship.

Unit Verse: My command is this: Love each other as I have loved you. John 15:12

Unit Affirmation: I CAN BE A FRIEND TO OTHERS AS JESUS IS A FRIEND TO ME!

PRINCIPLES...

Learning About Friendships

This unit will help Juniors understand several aspects of friendship. These include:

JESUS IS THE BEST FRIEND WE CAN HAVE.

In our world today, children learn early that human friendships are often confusing, disappointing and constantly changing. Your children will soon discover, if they haven't already, that friendships change for all kinds of reasons. When they do, we are left to deal with feelings of abandonment, betrayal, and just plain grief. During those times, it is easy for them to lose their ability to trust new friends because they fear they will only be hurt again. The greatest security we can give our children, therefore, is knowing that there is one constant, neverchanging relationship they can have. No matter what changes around them, Jesus will always be there and that's something they can count on!

JESUS IS OUR EXAMPLE OF WHAT IT MEANS TO BE A FRIEND TO OTHERS.

As we begin to understand our relationship to Jesus better, we can think about how knowing Him can help us be a good friend to others. Remember the Golden Rule, "Do Unto Others As You Would Have Them Do Unto You"? In this series of lessons, we want to put a new twist to that Golden Rule. "Treat others in the same way Jesus treats you!" There are many aspects of being a good friend we can learn in this way. Here are three your child will be discussing in the weeks ahead:

• Being a good friend means

including others in our circle of friends. Children at this age are very aware of the need to belong to the group. For many who feel outside of the group, however, life can be excruciatingly painful. Your children can learn to be sensitive to others around them, and how Jesus' example teaches us that everyone has the right to belong. Once they catch on, they will discover that including others enriches their friendships.

• Being a good friend means speaking to one another with respect and words of encouragement, not put-downs and words of anger. As they observe the examples of communication styles around them, our kids are often learning that put-downs, insults, and vindictiveness are the normal ways we speak to one another in our society. Your child can learn a better way by remembering Jesus' example. A simple little rule: "Say words that *help*, not *hurt*, and say them in a *kind* way."

• Being a good friend means keeping confidences. Everyone needs safe places to tell their secrets. Now is the time for your children to learn that being trusted with a friend's secret is a special privilege to be treasured and not violated. It's not always easy, but it is a very special part of being a good friend!

There is, however, one exception to this rule. When our friends tell us that they are being hurt in some way, we need to share that secret with someone who can help. At that point, our concern for our friend's safety is more important than keeping the confidence.

PRACTICE...

Learning About Friendships

Participating in one or more of the following activities will reinforce the principles of being a good friend presented in this unit.

1. PORTRAIT OF A FRIEND.

During dinner one night, ask everyone in your family to choose one person who s/he thinks is the most like Jesus. Ask each person to share who they chose, and why. Then talk about what you can learn about being a good friend from the examples of these people

2. WATCH TV TOGETHER

and look for characteristics of good friendships. Talk about the positive examples you see, and the negative examples. Do you see any of these traits, positive and negative, in yourselves?

3. INCLUDING OTHERS.

Help your children learn the value of opening up to new friends by designating a "new friend day" once every month. Ask your kids to invite someone they don't know very well over to play for the afternoon or evening. Encourage them to include those new friends they enjoy in more of their future activities.

Model including others by your life style, as well. Invite families you don't know well or who have a special need into your home on a regular basis. Be sure your children know you are reaching out to them because you, too, want to "be a friend to others as Jesus is to you!"

4. WHEN YOU ARE CONCERNED ABOUT YOUR CHILDREN'S CHOICE OF FRIENDS,

don't panic! Remember, this is an emotional issue for your children and criticizing or condemning their choice may only alienate them from you. Take the time to discuss the friends in question, being clear about your concerns and giving your children the chance to express their feelings. If the friendship continues, make some rules about it; i.e., you can only play at our house, certain games are off-limits, you may not use the same language s/he does, etc. You can maintain clear limits about your child's friendships without eliminating their choices.

Lesson 1

What Makes a Good Friend?

Aim: That your students will be good friends to others.

Scripture: Il Samuel 18:1-4

Unit Verse: My command is this: Love each other as I have loved you. John 15:12

Unit Affirmation: I CAN BE A FRIEND TO OTHERS AS JESUS IS A FRIEND TO ME!

 Planning Ahead

1. Photocopy activity sheets (pages 87 and 88)—one for each student.
2. Prepare the Unit Affirmation poster by writing the following on a large poster board: I CAN BE A FRIEND TO OTHERS AS JESUS IS A FRIEND TO ME! Add the numbers 1-5 vertically down the left-hand side.
3. Prepare five construction paper strips per student.

1 Setting the Stage (5-10 minutes)

WHAT YOU'LL DO

- Play a game to discover students' current attitudes about friendships

WHAT YOU'LL NEED

- A pair of dice or a spinner with twelve sections on it
- Copy of the friendship game questions

2 Introducing the Issue (20 minutes)

WHAT YOU'LL DO

- Complete an activity sheet that describes three different levels of friendship
- Introduce the Unit Affirmation Poster

WHAT YOU'LL NEED

- "Building Friendships" Activity Sheet (page 87)
- Paper and markers for Friendship Cartoons
- Unit Affirmation Poster

3 Searching the Scriptures (20 minutes)

WHAT YOU'LL DO

- Participate in a play about the friendship between David and Jonathan
- Make a paper "Friendship" chain

WHAT YOU'LL NEED

- Bibles
- "A Friendly Quantum Leap" Activity Sheet (page 88)
- Five construction paper strips per student
- Markers
- Glue

4 Living the Lesson (5-10 minutes)

WHAT YOU'LL DO

- Create a "telephone devotional" based on the Unit Verse

WHAT YOU'LL NEED

- Answering machine or tape recorder
- Bibles
- Concordance

 *Lesson 1*

 # Setting the Stage (5-10 minutes)

As students arrive, involve them in THE FRIENDSHIP GAME. **Today, we're going to begin a series on Friendship. Who is your best friend?** (Allow kids to respond.) **Can you tell me why you like them so much?** Some students may not be able to tell why they like their best friend. They just know they do! **Let's play a game to help us identify what we like about our friends and even some things that we wish were different.** To play, let kids take turns throwing the dice or spinning the spinner. Then, ask the student to answer the question below that corresponds to the number they threw (or spun). Encourage your students to think about their answers and give you honest feelings. **There are no right and wrong answers to these questions. I really want to know what you are thinking and feeling about friendships.** Encourage them to pay close attention to the attitudes about friendships they reveal as they answer these questions.

1. The MOST IMPORTANT quality of being a friend is_____.
2. I HATE IT when my friends_____.
3. Name one thing you have done to get friends.
4. I wish my friends would _____ more often.
5. Name two things you do to KEEP your friends.
6. Name two qualities that would make you NOT WANT TO BE FRIENDS with someone.
7. The HARDEST THING about having friends is_____.
8. Without friends, life would be_____.
9. When my parents DON'T LIKE my friends, I_____.
10. How many friends are "too many"?
11. I wish my friends would _____ less often.
12. What do you do when someone you want to be friends with DOES NOT want to be friends with you?

Continue with the game until all students have arrived and everyone has had a chance to answer at least one question.

 # Introducing the Issue (20 minutes)

Having friends is something we all want, but we can often have trouble doing well. Distribute copies of the activity sheet, "Building Friendships" (page 87), and explain that it will help us think about the different kinds of friends we have in our lives.

Refer students to the activity sheet, and look at the three building blocks on it. **Each block refers to a different level of friendship. When learning to be a good friend, it is important for us to remember that we all have different kinds of friends, and the characteristics of being a good friend are different**

Lesson 1 ✓

for each. Take a few minutes to decode the words that will identify the three levels of friendship.

Level 1 are <u>acquaintances</u>. **What is an acquaintance?** (Someone who we know by name, but don't see very often or spend much time with.) **How many acquaintances can you have?** (As many as you want.) **Since acquaintances don't take much time, we usually have a lot.**

Look at the characteristics listed on the right-hand side of the paper. Which characteristics are needed to be a good friend to an acquaintance? Let kids look over the list and respond. Have them put a "1" in the box next to the following characteristics.

- Smile and be pleasant
- Give compliments when appropriate
- Include them in conversation when they are close by
- Offer help in small ways

Level 2 are <u>good friends</u>. **When we find acquaintances we would like to get to know better, we move into the second level of friendship. How many good friends can a person have?** About 6-8. Explain that being a good friend takes more time and energy, and therefore there are limits on how many we can have. Although there is no rule about it, most of us cannot be a good friend to more than 6–8 people at one time.

Look again at the characteristics list on the right. What characteristics do you think are appropriate for this level of friendship? Help them see that this is a deeper level of relationship, and therefore demands more commitment from us. Have them put a "2" in the boxes next to the following characteristics:

- Invite them to do things with you
- Give help when it is needed and you are available
- Take an interest in the things that interest them
- Share some personal information
- Notice what they need and help them get it
- Keep private information they share with you to yourself

Level 3 are <u>best friends</u>. **One of the most satisfying parts of life is having best friends! How many best friends can a person have?** Probably one or two. Help your kids see that being a *best* friend is a big commitment that takes *lots* of time and energy. None of us can have more than two at one time, and still do a good job of it.

Look at the remaining characteristics on the right-hand side. Place a "3" in the box next to the characteristic of a best friend.

- Spend lots of time with them
- Share private thoughts and feelings
- *Really* listen to the other person
- Encourage them to be the best they can be
- Protect them, when necessary
- Drop everything to help in a crisis

•Consider the other's feelings and desires as much as my own

Divide your class into groups of 2-3 (they will probably want to with their friends), and give each group paper and markers. **As a group, choose a characteristic of a friend which you think is one of the *most important* ones. Then, design a short (1-3 frames) cartoon illustrating this characteristic.** Explain that they can use stick figures and dialogue balloons to create the action. When they are finished, have each group share their cartoon with the rest of the class.

Display the Unit Affirmation Poster that has I CAN BE A FRIEND TO OTHERS AS JESUS IS A FRIEND TO ME! written across the top and the numbers 1-5 written vertically along the left-hand side. Make sure everyone can see it and you can write on it easily. **We have been talking about what makes a good friend. Some people sum up what it means to be a good friend in a rule which we call, "The Golden Rule." Does anyone know what the Golden Rule says?** Allow for responses. **The Golden Rule is: "Do unto others as you would have them do unto you." That says a lot about being a good friend, but our Unit Affirmation for this unit says even more.** Ask the class to read aloud the Affirmation together. Encourage the kids to see that there is no better friend anywhere than the kind of friend Jesus is to us. We can learn a lot about being a friend by following His teachings and example.

Think for a moment about the characteristics of a good friend that we talked about today, and about the kind of friend Jesus is to us. What do you think we could write on the first line of our poster that tells us how we can be a friend like Jesus? Let kids give ideas. Possibilities may include: Be committed to the other person; Care about the feelings of others; Give of yourself.

After a few minutes of discussion, agree on one phrase and write it on the poster. **Now let's look at God's Word to discover more about being a good friend!**

Searching the Scriptures (20 minutes)

Almost everyone agrees s/he wants to have at least one good friend. People in Bible times felt the same way. You've already discussed some of the characteristics of a good friend, but now let's see what being a good friend involves. Introduce study by explaining "Quantum Leap" as follows: **During an experiment about time something strange happens and scientist Dr. Scram Beckett is zapped back in time. Directed there by an authoritative power source he finds himself sent to different periods of history. In each situation Scram has been sent back to replace someone of that time period and help out people involved in a problem. Instead of appearing like a stranger, when other people see or hear him he looks and sounds like the person he has been sent to replace. An assistant, Pal, is there to help Scram. He is invisible and inaudible to everyone but Scram. Another helper, Ziggy, is a master computer that provides historical information needed to help Scram adjust to his new situation.**

Pass out copies of "A Friendly Quantum Leap" activity sheet (page 88). **Now, let's**

Lesson 1 ✔

see what a good friend looks like in action. Since this story is done as a play, you will need people to take the parts of Saul, Eliab, Scram, Pal, and Jonathan. The rest of the class can act out the actions of the crowd. Choose someone with a mature voice to be Saul. Jonathan should be played by someone who is warm and outgoing.

Why did Jonathan give David his sword and clothes? (He wanted to show his friendship to David; he believed David would be the next king of Israel.) Jonathan knew that having a loving relationship with God was the most important thing in life. His loyalty to the Lord enabled him to reach out in love to David. Because he knew God loved him and would be his forever friend, Jonathan was able to put the welfare of others ahead of his personal well-being. He recognized David was God's choice for king and did all he could to promote David. Without hesitation Jonathan declared his complete, unquestioning, loyal friendship to David. He decided he would rather lose his throne than lose his friendship with David.

The friendship between Jonathan and David was an important part of their lives. If they were to give a definition of friendship, they might say that a good friend is loyal. How would you complete the sentence; A good friend_____? (Your students may have a variety of endings for this sentence including such aspects as these: loving and caring for others; being loyal; taking time to listen; sharing; helping.)

Friendship can be costly. **What did his friendship with David cost Jonathan?** (It cost him his throne and kingly inheritance, grief and sadness, and even put his life in jeopardy as he acted as peacemaker between David and Saul.) **Have you ever had to give up something for a friend?** Allow time for your students to share their experiences. By sharing an experience you have had you can open up the discussion and help your kids identify with you.

What are some things that break relationships between people and nations? Some of these items are: greed; differences in customs, culture, appearances, ages; telling secrets; selfishness; mistrust or fear. Someone once described friendship as the world's strongest glue. **How can broken relationships be mended by being a good friend to others?** The positive actions of loyalty, unconditional love, sharing, nurturing, and two-way communication all tear down barriers and replace them with bridges.

Jesus gave us a perfect example of a good friend as He loved and cared for people. He also told us how we can be a good friend to others. Have someone read the Unit Verse, "My command is this: Love one another as I have loved you." John 15:12. **How did Jonathan demonstrate this kind of love through his friendship with David?** (He shared with him, treated him like his brother, was loyal to him.) **What are some ways you can show love to a friend?** Let students share specific ways.

Most of us would like to have Jonathan for a friend. Why? There are many benefits to be gained through such a loving relationship with a good friend like

Jonathan. **Do you think Jonathan would like to have you as his friend?** There is an old saying, "To have a friend, be a friend." While everybody would probably like to have Jonathan as a friend, not everyone is willing to take the time and effort to be the same kind of good friend he was. It has been pointed out that friendship is the only relationship which is based on mutual desire alone. Friends can turn away from their relationship anytime they want to. Friendship is a two-way street. We will find the more friendly we are, the more friends we have.

Pass out five strips of colored construction paper to each student. Ask a volunteer to look up Ephesians 4:2 and read it aloud. **After hearing this verse, write on your paper strips ideas for ways to be a good friend.** For example: Forgive your friend when s/he asks you to; Don't use put-downs; Spend time with your friend; Encourage your friend when s/he's blue; Don't ignore your friend when you are with others; Put your friend's happiness ahead of your own.

Let the kids glue the links together into a "Friendship Chain." Decorate your room or bulletin board with it. Point out how real, active friendship links people together.

Living the Lesson (5-10 Minutes)

For fun, let's create a friendship reminder to use with the tool that keeps a lot of friends linked together -- the telephone! Let your students create a "telephone devotional" by using the Unit Verse or Ephesians 4:32 along with several timely tips from the students' friendship links. Because this devotional is to be designed so people can just call a number and listen to the message, it needs to be kept brief. A simple format might be: Unit Verse or other Scripture; brief statement telling how Jonathan showed that kind of love to David; two or three tips on how to be a good friend; a closing sentence prayer. Let kids take turns giving different parts of this devotional. Although you might not actually use the devotional on a telephone you can add to the reality of this activity by taping the message. Your students will love hearing themselves as the tape is played back.

> **Optional:** If desired, you might want to inquire about renting or using a phone line for a few weeks so other kids or church members could take advantage of this recorded devotional.

Close with prayer asking God to help each of you become better friends. Give each student two candies. One is for them and one is to be shared with a friend.

Building Friendships

Level # 3: BTES FEDRINS

_____

How many can I have?_____

_____

_____

_____

Level #2: DOGO SFIRDEN

_____

How many can I have? _____

_____

_____

_____

Level # 1: ASETIQCANUACN

_____

How many can I have? _____

_____

_____

_____

- ☐ Smile and be pleasant
- ☐ Take an interest in things that interest them
- ☐ Protect them, when necessary
- ☐ Give compliments when appropriate
- ☐ Include them in conversation when they are close by
- ☐ Share some personal information
- ☐ Keep private information they share with you to yourself
- ☐ Drop everything to help in a crisis
- ☐ Encourage them to be the best they can be
- ☐ Invite them to do things with you
- ☐ Offer help in small ways
- ☐ Spend lots of time with them
- ☐ Share private thoughts and feelings
- ☐ Give help when it is needed and you are available
- ☐ Notice what they need and help them get it
- ☐ Consider the other's feelings and desires as much as your own
- ☐ _Really_ listen to the other person

A Friendly Quantum Leap

(Crowd of people surround Saul, Scram, and Jonathan)

SAUL: Didn't you hear, me young man? I asked you whose son you are.

SCRAM: Yes, sir, I heard you. (looks around, bewildered) I'm the son of . . . the son of . . . (Eliab steps forward from crowd).

ELIAB: The son of your servant Jesse of Bethlehem, my king. David is a bit mixed up after his great victory. He's a great warrior and my brother! (proudly hugs Scram around shoulders; crowd cheers)

PAL (appears out of crowd; everyone freezes except Pal and Scram): You almost blew it that time, Scram.

SCRAM: Pal! Boy, am I glad to see you! Where am I? Who is this David?

PAL (consulting calculator in hand): It seems you're in Israel about a thousand years before Jesus was born. You're David, a kid who's been a sheepherder since he could toddle. Although he's a shrimp in size, he's a terrific athlete. He also trusts God to help him do things. Ziggy (looks at calculator) says he's already killed a bear and a lion. And now he's just killed Goliath, Israel's enemy who's a giant over nine feet tall. It's no wonder Eliab is so proud of you! Hey, see that handsome kid over there, the one with the fancy robe, belt, and weapons? That's Jonathan, Saul's son. I think he wants to talk to you. (Pal steps to side; Jonathan steps up to Scram; others look on)

JONATHAN: David, do you remember me?

SCRAM: You're the prince, Jonathan. You know who I am?

JONATHAN: Of course. Ever since you played the harp to quiet my father's bad moods, I've been hoping you'd come back. You were very brave to kill Goliath, David. How did you dare to challenge him?

SCRAM: I did it because I knew God would help me. I knew I could trust His strength and guidance. He's my best friend.

JONATHAN: That's just how I feel about God, too. David, I want to be your friend as long as I live. Here, I want to give you a present. (Takes off coat, belt, bow, arrows, and sword and gives them to Scram) Please accept these to show you will be my friend. I believe God has called you to be Israel's next king.

SCRAM: They're wonderful gifts, but I can't take them. I'm only a shepherd and not a prince. I don't know what to say. (Pal steps over to Scram; all others freeze)

PAL: Just say "Thanks," and you'd better believe they're wonderful gifts, Scram. Only King Saul and Prince Jonathan have iron swords. That sword you're holding is the most highly prized weapon in Israel. Not only are those the royal robes (looks at calculator), but according to the customs here, by giving them to you, Jonathan means that he is giving up his inherited position so you can become the next king.

SCRAM: Wow, he really likes me! (Pal steps aside; characters resume actions) Thank you, Prince Jonathan. I'll be happy to be your friend.

JONATHAN (helps Scram put on coat): Call me Jonathan. Then it's settled. We will be like brothers. No matter what happens, David, I'll be loyal to you. You can count on me because you mean more to me than anyone else except God.

SCRAM: I'll be faithful to you too. We'll be friends as long as we live, Jonathan. (Scram and Jonathan hug each other.)

Lesson 2

You Don't Belong!

Aim: That your students will abandon cliques and pattern their friendships after God's all-inclusive love.

Scripture: Luke 10:25-37

Unit Verse: My command is this: Love each other as I have loved you. John 15:12

Unit Affirmation: I CAN BE A FRIEND TO OTHERS AS JESUS IS A FRIEND TO ME!

✓ Planning Ahead

1. Copy roleplays from SEARCHING THE SCRIPTURES onto index cards.
2. Post six 12" x 18" pieces of paper around the room with these headings:
   - My Favorite Food
   - My Favorite Subject in School
   - My Favorite Sport
   - My Favorite Hobby
   - My Favorite Holiday
   - My Favorite TV Show
3. Write out these instructions for making a Name Banner:
   Make a Name Banner
   - Print your name in big letters in the middle of a piece of paper.
   - Around your name, use pictures and words to illustrate some of your favorite things.
   - Add a border or other finishing touches.
4. Photocopy activity sheets (pages 95 and 96)—one for each student.

1 | Setting the Stage (5-10 minutes)

WHAT YOU'LL DO

- Participate in an activity to introduce the subject of cliques

WHAT YOU'LL NEED

- "My Favorite Things" posters
- Materials for name banners
- Treats for everyone in the class
- Tape

2 | Introducing the Issue (20 minutes)

WHAT YOU'LL DO

- Discuss why we form cliques and the problems they cause
- Make anti–clique picket signs and display some around the room
- Add a phrase to the Unit Affirmation Poster

WHAT YOU'LL NEED

- "Anti–Clique Campaign" Activity Sheet (page 95)
- Markers
- Unit Affirmation Poster

3 | Searching the Scriptures (20 minutes)

WHAT YOU'LL DO

- Roleplay ways to be sensitive to those who need a friend
- Dramatize a story that shows how God wants people to be friends with others

WHAT YOU'LL NEED

- "A Friend Indeed" Activity Sheet (page 96)
- Copies of roleplays written on index cards
- Bibles

4 | Living the Lesson (5-10 minutes)

WHAT YOU'LL DO

- Add to the "telephone devotional"

WHAT YOU'LL NEED

- Tape recorder

 Setting the Stage (5-10 minutes)

Before the kids arrive, post the six "favorite things" posters around the room. On a table, lay out additional pieces of paper and markers, with the "Make a Name Banner" instructions (See Planning Ahead).

As we continue our series on friendships, we want to get to know the friends in our class. Take some time to visit each of the posters that are hanging up and write your name and favorite item as listed on the top of the poster. Explain that when they have visited all the posters, they can go to the table and make a name banner, following the directions on the table.

As the kids are working, make note of the items they have listed on the posters. Then, choose a few items that you can use to "eliminate" about one fourth of your class. For instance, you might choose those who said math was their favorite subject in school, and those who listed chocolate pudding as their favorite food. There should be no logic to the selections you make.

When most are finished with their name banners, give the following instructions: **It's time to move on with our lesson, so I would like you to take your name banners, put them up around the room and then join me over at this table. Oh, that is except for those of you who said that math was your favorite subject, or chocolate pudding was your favorite food. I want you to take your name banners and stand in the back of the room.**

When everyone has finished following those instructions, congratulate the group sitting with you around the table for doing an excellent job, and give each one a treat. You can be certain that protests will be voiced from the "outside" group. **I think it's only right that anyone who likes math or chocolate pudding *not* be allowed to have a treat. What's wrong with that?**

Allow the kids to express their feelings about being on the outside, about being in the "privileged" group, and about the unfairness of the criteria for who is left out. At this point, keep the discussion short. End it by "giving in" and inviting the "outsiders" to display their banners and join the rest of the class. Don't forget to give them their treats!

 Introducing the Issue (20 minutes)

You can debrief the activity by discussing the following questions. **What does it feel like to be left out?** Let the outsiders share their feelings and then give an opportunity for anyone to share a time when they felt left out of something. **When it comes to friendships, do we ever have "insiders" and**

"outsiders"? **What is that called?** (Cliques.) **What are some reasons why we form cliques?** (It's hard to include everyone; we want to feel like we belong; human nature; etc.) **In our game, liking math and chocolate pudding were silly reasons for excluding people from our group. What are some real reasons why we exclude others from joining our cliques?** (They are new; they don't look "right"; not good at a certain sport or activity; too smart or too dumb; etc.) **Are cliques helpful to our relationships, or harmful?** Help the kids see that although forming cliques seems natural, they are harmful both to those *in* the clique as much as those *outside* the clique. **What are the harmful results of having cliques?** (People get hurt; you might have to do things you don't want to do just to keep being accepted by the group; you miss out on making new and interesting friends by never getting to know anyone new; etc.)

Forming cliques is a natural thing that happens all the time. At first, it may seem exciting to be accepted in one. But after a while, we can begin to see that cliques are hurtful to others *and* to ourselves. Hurting others and cutting ourselves off from new people and experiences is *never* a good way to live! As Christians, we have the power to choose a better way! Although it may be hard at first, we can choose to reach out to others and include them in our circle of friends and acquaintances.

Distribute copies of the activity sheet, "Anti–Clique Campaign" (page 95). **What do people do when they want to tell others to *stop* a harmful action, like taking drugs or polluting the environment?** Allow for responses before continuing. They wage an anti–whatever campaign by making TV commercials, putting up posters, and any other means they can think of to get their message across. Sometimes, they make picket signs and go places to demonstrate in favor of their cause.

Today, we are going to promote our own, "Anti–Clique Campaign" by making picket signs. Let's think of some ideas for our signs.

Get the creative process started by suggesting one or two ideas. Once they get the idea, encourage them to create their own slogans to put on their activity sheets. Some slogan suggestions include: Cliques hurt everyone!; No cliques here! (with a "NO" sign over the word "clique"); Try something new. . . take a new friend to McDonald's; This could be YOU –> (a picture of one person standing outside a group of others).

When the students are finished with their activity sheets, refer to the Unit Affirmation Poster and ask kids to read the affirmation out loud together. Review the phrase you added last week and what it means. **Jesus is a perfect example of how we can have a group of our own friends, but not be a clique. Even though He had His close friends (the 12 disciples), He knew**

how to include others in very special ways. **Can you think of times when Jesus made some people feel included who were excluded by everyone else around them?** (Share examples such as Zacchaeus, healing lepers and crippled people, calling the children to Him when the disciples wanted to send them away, etc.)

Thinking about Jesus' example, what phrase could we add to our poster today? (Possibilities include: Everyone is welcome; Don't worry about what others say; Reach out and touch someone.)

Jesus not only taught us how to treat others by the way He lived; He also talked about it. What did He say? Let's find out!

Searching the Scriptures (20 minutes)

Do you think they had cliques in Bible times? Kids probably think of Bible people as having lived so long ago that they never had the problems we do today. **Let's find out.** Have someone read the story of the Good Samaritan from Luke 10:25-37.

What was the response of the priest and the Levite? (They walked on by and wouldn't get involved.) **Who was the neighbor or friend in the story?** (The Samaritan.) **Do you know why it was a surprise to those listening to the story that the Samaritan was the good neighbor?** The kids may not realize that in Jesus' day the Jews and the Samaritans did not get along at all. The Jews thought that they were much better than the Samaritans and would go out of their way to avoid the Samaritans. Thus, when the wounded Jewish traveler was helped by a Samaritan, it was quite a surprise!

It's a good thing people don't act like that today. Or do they? Maybe we should take a look at a modern situation to find out for sure. Hand out copies of "A Friend Indeed" activity sheet (page 96). It is a junior-age paraphrase of this parable. For this skit you will need five students to play the main parts. Other kids can be the gang members and also join in to answer Jesus' question at the end of the play.

Give the kids a little bit of time to look over their parts and then act out the scenario. **How was this play like the story Jesus told?** Allow time for your students to compare the actions of the various characters. You may want to help them with some leading questions. **Who was Suz Smart like?** (The priest.) **Did Jon Jock remind you of anyone in Jesus' story?** (The Levite.) **What did Suz and Jon have in common?** (They were both interested in only their own friends and plans.)

How was Ned like the Samaritan? (He stopped, cared for the wounds; helped the wounded person to a place where someone would take care of

him, paid for things he needed, helped someone who had kept him out of his circle of friends.) **Ken admitted that he and his friends made fun of Ned. Because the clique treated him that way, how do you think Ned felt?** (Sad; left out; angry; lonely; wanted to get even.) **How might Ned have felt when he saw Ken was hurt and in trouble?** (Glad; thought it served him right for the way he had treated Ned.) **What could Ned have done when he saw Ken's predicament?** (Made fun of him; taken advantage of him and beaten up on him more; ignored him and passed by like Suz and Jon.) **Why did Ned say he helped Ken?** (Because he needed a friend.)

How do you think this situation might affect Ken's thoughts about friendship? (He might try to be a better friend, understand how a good friend should act, try to include more people in his friendships.) Help your students understand that friendship shouldn't be based on the job we have, the social position we hold, our looks or talents. Jesus chose His close friends from common, uneducated, working-class people. These people were looked down upon by the wealthy, "beautiful" people of their day. But Jesus saw these fishermen, tax collectors, and street people as individuals who needed and wanted friendship. They gladly accepted Jesus' friendship and offered Him their own. Those people who were self-centered and clique-oriented had a difficult, if not impossible, time accepting His friendship because they felt no need of it or thought He should only have friends like themselves. Jesus told this parable to open their eyes to the opportunities for friendship which lay all around them.

How do you think Ken might treat Ned in the future? (He might stop making fun of him; tell his friends that Ned was a good person and deserved their friendship; try to get his friends to include Ned, too.) **Do you think Ken might feel differently about Suz and Jock after this situation? How?** There is nothing like a difficult situation to highlight who our real friends are. The persons who remain or become our friends when we are in need are our true friends indeed!

This is the kind of friendship Jesus refers to in our Unit Verse, John 15:12. He offers everyone a friendship that was based on an unconditional, all-inclusive love. In His opinion all people are God's creations and worthy of His love and friendship. He gave His life to confirm that conviction.

To further illustrate the need to break down harmful cliques do some "all in the point of view" roleplays. Kids will roleplay situations from two different viewpoints. First, they will do it from the viewpoint of someone needing a friend. Then the situation is repeated from the viewpoint of the other person involved who is sensitive to the problem and willing to help.

Wait until both viewpoints are acted out before discussing them. Talk about

the feelings of each character and how they might change as the viewpoints change. **What problems did the cliques cause? How can kids be alert to the needs of others and what can they do to extend friendship to them?**

1. Linda is new in school. Tammie is in the same grade and has noticed her, but has been busy with her own friends. Viewpoint 1: Linda feels lonely and leftout. Linda thinks, "I wish I had a friend." Viewpoint 2: "It must be hard to be a stranger. How can I help her?" Tammie wonders.

2. Randy has been captain of the team and he and the other players are always together. Rick is the water boy and takes care of the equipment. He knows that he isn't athletic enough to ever be on the team. Viewpoint 1: "I wish I could do something with them sometime," Rick dreams. Viewpoint 2: Randy asks himself, "How can we include Rick in our fun?"

3. Paula's parents are divorced and she lives with her mom and older sister. There isn't much money and she often has to wear her sister's hand-me-downs. Michelle wears designer clothes and so do her friends. Viewpoint 1: "I could be their friend, too, if they'd just let me," Paula thinks. "I can't help it because I don't dress like they do." Viewpoint 2: Michelle wonders, "Paula looks sad. Maybe she would like to talk to a friend."

4. Chris and Kirk were good friends. Both enjoy music. This year Chris sings in the choir and Kirk plays in the band. They see very little of each other anymore because each one is busy in his own music group. Viewpoint 1: Chris thinks, "I sure miss Kirk. I sure wish he'd taken choir instead of band. He doesn't have time for me now." Viewpoint 2: "I miss Chris. I wonder if he ever thinks about me?" Kirk ponders. "Maybe I should find out how he's doing."

✔ Living the Lesson (5-10 minutes)

To wrap up today's lesson, record another "telephone devotional." Have students say the Unit Verse together and suggest some ways they can show this kind of love by patterning their friendships after God's all-inclusive love. Select two or three of these suggestions, the Unit Verse or Romans 15:7 and a sentence prayer for the devotional. Let kids record it.

Close today's session by singing a verse of "We Are One in the Spirit" and a group hug.

Anti-Clique Campaign ✓

Design an anti–clique slogan and draw it in the picket sign below.

✔ A Friend Indeed

Cast: Ken Kool (one of the "in" crowd); Suz Smart (member of the student counsel); Jon Jock (the school star athlete); Ned Nerd (wears thick glasses which he keeps pushing up on his nose); several members of a street gang; narrator.

Scene: A filthy alley a few blocks from school.

Narrator: Ken Kool was on his way to school one day. (Ken enters riding bike) On the way some muggers stole his money and his racing-pro bike and beat him up. (Gang members enter, grab billfold and bike, beat Ken up, then run off) Then they left him lying in the alley. (Ken moans loudly) It happened that Suz Smart passed the alley on her way to student counsel and saw Ken.

Suz (Enters businesslike): Oh, gross! I sure don't want to get involved. I could break a nail or mess up my hair. Why, I might even get mugged! Besides, I've got to hurry or I'll be late for student counsel meeting. (Dashes off; Ken moans again)

Narrator: She crossed the street and walked by on the other side. Next it happened that Jon Jock came by. He went over and looked at Ken.

Jon (Swaggers over): What's happenin', Dude? Yo, they nailed you good. What a bummer! Well, I've got to get to practice; I'm the star and they can't do without me. Have a good one! (Lopes off; Ken groans louder)

Narrator: Jon crossed the street and walked by on the other side. Then Ned Nerd came down the same street. He saw Ken and went over to him.

Ned (Enters pushing bike. Rushes over to Ken, puts bike kickstand down and kneels by him): Wow! How awful! Are you all right, Ken? Here, let me help you. Where does it hurt? (Takes out handkerchief and wipes some of the dirt off Ken's wounds. Fishes in pocket and pulls out a slightly crumpled Band-aid) Here, Mom always said this would come in handy some day. (Puts it on Ken; pushes glasses up on nose)

Ken (Looks at Ned in amazement): Aren't you the jerk my friends and I always make fun of? Why are you helping me?

Ned (Matter of factly): Because you need help.

Ken: But don't you hate me for the way I've mistreated you? You could have gone right on by just like everybody else did.

Ned: No, I couldn't. You need a friend right now. Lean on me and I'll help you get on my bike. (Ned helps Ken struggle to his feet. Leaning on Ned, Ken manages to get on the bike.)

Ken: Where are you taking me?

Ned: To the school nurse. (Both exit with Ned pushing Ken on bike)

Narrator: Ned took Ken to the nurse and stayed to see he would be okay. (Ned and Ken enter. Ned helps Ken sit down; then takes money out of his jeans pocket.)

Ned: Here's some lunch money. It isn't much, but at least you won't starve.

Ken: You're gonna be late for math.

Ned: That's not important right now. (Pushes glasses up on nose) What's important is helping you out. (Ken shakes head and stares at him in wonder.)

Narrator: Then Jesus said, "Which one of these kids was a friend to Ken?"

All (shout): The one who helped him.

Narrator: Jesus said to them, "Then go and do the same."

Lesson 3

Get Off My Case!

Aim: That your students will stop criticizing and saying put-downs to each other but instead, support each other.

Scripture: Numbers 12:1-15

Unit Verse: My command is this: Love each other as I have loved you. John 15:12

Unit Affirmation: I CAN BE A FRIEND TO OTHERS AS JESUS IS A FRIEND TO ME!

 Planning Ahead

1. Gather the following materials for the tin punch project in SETTING THE STAGE: Disposable aluminum pie plates (6" or 9"); One hammer and one large nail for each child; two old magazines for each child; masking tape; tin punch patterns (You can make these by taking a simple outlined object, such as a star or butterfly from a coloring book, and drawing a large dot about every half inch all around the design. This will tell the kids where to pound the nails.)
2. Using a purple marker, draw a grape cluster on a large sheet of paper.
3. Photocopy activity sheets (pages 103 and 104)—one for each student.

1 Setting the Stage (5-10 minutes)

WHAT YOU'LL DO

- Make a tin punch project as an object lesson about the power of words

WHAT YOU'LL NEED

- Materials for the tin punch project (See Planning Ahead)

2 Introducing the Issue (20 minutes)

WHAT YOU'LL DO

- Make Friendship Affirmation Cards to reinforce the power of positive words
- Add a phrase to the Unit Affirmation Poster
- Discuss the power of put-downs and identify where people learn them
- Consider ways they can support their friends

WHAT YOU'LL NEED

- "Words of Friendship" Activity Sheet (page 103)
- Unit Affirmation Poster

3 Searching the Scriptures (20 minutes)

WHAT YOU'LL DO

- Discover how criticizing others hurts us as well as them

WHAT YOU'LL NEED

- Bibles
- "Unsolved Mysteries" Activity Sheet (page 104)
- Large sheet of newsprint and purple marker or crayon

4 Living the Lesson (5-10 minutes)

WHAT YOU'LL DO

- Add to the "telephone devotional"

WHAT YOU'LL NEED

- Bibles
- Tape recorder
- Optional: Purple happy-face sticker for each student

 *Lesson 3*

Setting the Stage (5-10 minutes)

Before the kids arrive, set up the project by placing two old magazines, one pie plate, one pattern, and one nail at each place. When your students arrive greet each one. **Today we are going to take a look at a way that we can impact others or make an impression on them. Can you think of a person who has really made an impression on your life?** Encourage the kids to think of someone who has influenced their lives either in a positive or negative way. **What did that person do to impact your life in such a big way?** Allow kids to share briefly.

We're going to work on an activity that will make a big impression—on these pie plates! Instruct the kids to tape the pattern inside the pie plate, and tape it securely in place. Then, they are to hammer the nail through each dot on the pattern, being sure it makes a hole all the way through the pie plate, but does *not* go through the magazines (no holes in the table, please!). When they

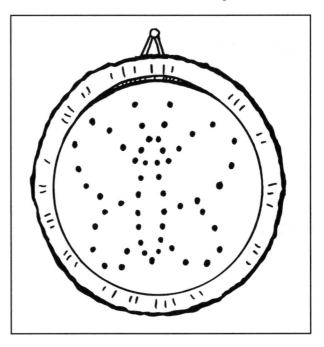

have punched through all the dots, they can remove the pattern and hold the plate up to the light, revealing the design they punched with the nail!

Important: When you clean up from this activity, keep the magazines with the holes in them in a stack near-by, as you will be referring to them as an object lesson during the discussion time.

Introducing the Issue (20 minutes)

One of the most powerful ways to impact another person or make an impression on someone is with the words we use. Tell the kids that in today's lesson we are going to be talking about the power words have in our friendships. **Perhaps you've never thought about it, but *what* we say to**

each other, and *how* we say it has tremendous power! We have the power to make others feel good and loved, or hurt them deeply just by the words we say. The problem is that many times we say things without thinking and we hurt our friends whether we meant to or not!

Can you think of some sayings about the power of words? (Let kids respond. Possibilities: Words can cut like a knife; I felt like someone punched me in the stomach; that really took the wind out of my sails, etc.)

Remember the old saying, "Sticks and stones can break my bones, but names will never hurt me!"? Is it true? (No; being called names hurts a lot)

Would anyone like to share a time they were called a name, or verbally put down in some way by a friend? (This is sensitive and kids may not want to share. If you have an example from your own life, share it at this time.)

Sometimes we will say, "Oh, I didn't really mean that!" after we have said something hurtful. Does that take the hurt away? (Although it may ease the sting, it doesn't take away the hurt of having been put down in the first place.)

Pick up several of the magazines that now have holes in them from the tin punch exercise. **Words are so powerful, we can't control the amount of hurt they can cause! It's like the tin punch activity we did today. I brought all these old magazines and it doesn't matter that they are now full of holes. But, suppose I had goofed, and brought my (wife's, mother's, dad's, roommate's) new magazines; ones they hadn't even read yet. I'd be in trouble when they found out, and I would feel just terrible! I would probably apologize all over the place, and hope they would forgive me. But you know what? I could *never* make these magazines the same as they were. I can *never* get rid of the effects of the nails being pounded in.**

Explain that our words are just like that. No matter how sorry we may be for saying something hurtful, we can never take the words back. The damage that has been done will remain.

Now ask the kids to make a list of the put-downs they say to each other, as you write them on the blackboard. To get them started, suggest one or two you have heard them say to each other during class time. Then, ask them to identify where they learned each one. Possible sources may be at home, from others on the playground, and on TV shows. Media is a significant source. Help them see that what may sound funny on a TV show or in a movie, can hurt deeply when used in a real-life situation.

No matter how innocently you may say a put-down to someone else, it is *never* right to hurt another person! As we learn to be friends as Jesus teaches

us, we can learn a better way to communicate!

Distribute copies of the activity sheet, "Words of Friendship." Instruct kids that just as words have power to hurt, they have just as much power to heal and help others feel good inside. Everyone likes to hear words that make them feel good, but it takes practice to learn to communicate with "words of friendship." Today, they will have a chance to say some special words to their friends by sending them a card. It's fun to get notes, and sometimes it's easier to say things in writing than it is face-to-face.

Kids can cut the cards apart, and then identify a person they can send each one to, with a special note written on the back. As they work, remind them that the power of words to *encourage* others is just as strong as the power to *discourage* them through put-downs. As time allows, they can color and decorate the cards.

Refer to the Unit Affirmation Poster again this week, and have the class read it through together. Remind them that Jesus teaches us to be friends by using words that help, not hurt. Ask for ideas for a phrase to add this week. Possibilities: Use words that help; Be an encourager!

The temptation to use put-downs is not new! Now let's look at some Bible people who had trouble with this same problem thousands of years ago.

 # Searching the Scriptures (20 minutes)

Turn to Numbers 12:1-15 and ask several volunteers to take turns reading the passage. **The Bible says that Miriam and Aaron spoke against Moses. What did they say?** (He had married a woman who was not a Hebrew; He's not the only person God speaks through.) **How do you think Moses felt about Miriam and Aaron's put-down?** (Sad; angry; hurt; upset.) Moses had grown up apart from his brother and sister. In obedience to God he had taken on a great place of leadership which caused an even greater gap between him and his family. He was lonely and in need of friendship. But in this story we find that instead of meeting his need in love and understanding, Miriam and Aaron united against their brother. **Have you ever felt like Moses did?** Ask volunteers to share times they had to deal with criticism.

Were Aaron and Miriam really angry about Moses' wife? (Although they may have been somewhat upset about her not being a Jew, it was not considered a sin to be married to an outsider until some time after the Exodus.) **What do you think the real reason was for their criticism?** They were jealous of Moses' influence among the Jews. Perhaps Miriam thought back to childhood and reasoned that if it had not been for her careful watching over her baby brother, he would not even be alive. Now his wife had taken Miriam's place in Moses' life. And Aaron found his little brother now had authority over him. Instead of dealing with their own feelings of inferiority and envy Miriam and Aaron attacked him through criticism. They created a sort of diversion to hide the real problem—their own sins of envy and resentment. Although they expressed their displeasure with Moses, they were also inwardly angry at God because of Moses' special relationship with Him.

Why do you think kids use put-downs? Often, like Miriam and Aaron we try to shift attention from our problems or feelings of inadequacy by raising a smoke screen which attacks a person's character instead of facing the real issue. Put-downs and criticism are forms of that kind of a fake-out.

What happened to Miriam as a result of her criticism? (God scolded her and punished her with temporary leprosy.) **How did Aaron feel about his and Miriam's behavior?** (He admitted they were foolish and had hurt Moses, his wife, and most of all God.) It's always easier to recognize foolish behavior after we have done it, but it's very hard to undo the harm we have caused by it. Aaron made a start in the right direction by asking for forgiveness and begging Moses to pray for Miriam's healing. Although God clearly demonstrated His displeasure with her behavior, He combined His discipline with loving mercy. She was restored to normal after seven days.

How do you feel after you have said a put-down? (Most kids will admit they really don't feel glad or better.) **How do you think the person you criticized feels?** (Sad; ashamed; inferior; angry.) **How do you think others who overheard the put-down feel about you?** (That you are only trying to find fault; afraid you'll treat them the same; think you're mean; maybe imitate you.)

How do you feel when you have said something kind and built someone up? (Happy; glad that I did something helpful.) **How do you think the person you encouraged feels?** (Glad; worthwhile; friendly; thankful.) **How do you think others who overheard your encouragement feel about you?** (That you are someone they would like as a friend; you're a neat person; maybe imitate you.) **Do you think criticizing others ever really builds anyone up? Why or why not?** (No. Put-downs only tear everybody down—the people who use it, those who hear it, and its victims.)

Pass out copies of the activity sheet "Unsolved Mysteries" (page 104). Your students will be detectives uncovering crimes of "Verbicide"—crimes of the tongue. They will also decide who the criminals are and the results of each crime. Allow time for kids to work on these problems individually then discuss them together. Follow a pattern similar to the following one for your discussion time.

Who is the criminal in the first mystery? (Mike.) **What crime was committed?** (Mike teased Bob about his learning disability.) **What do you think the results from this crime might be?** (Mike might lose Bob's friendship; Bob might find it hard to trust Mike with anything personal, fearing that Mike might throw it back at him when Mike's angry; Bob's self-esteem may go down if he thinks one of his best friends thinks he dumb.)

How could Mike make amends to Bob and support Bob? As students discuss ways they can support their friends, have them come up and use a purple marker to write their suggestions on grapes in the cluster you drew before class. Talk about ways to prevent this crime from happening again.

Why not start an "I heard it through the grapevine" club in your class? Whenever kids hear something good about someone they can tell that person and pass it on. They say, "I heard something good about you today!" then tell or show something good the person did or what someone else said good about that person. Your class can become a "grape" group by passing on good things about others.

Repeat the Unit Verse in unison. **How does this verse apply to put-downs?** Let kids think about how Jesus loves them. His love is steady and just. While He rebukes us for our sin, He never confuses the person with the act. Ask a volunteer to read Ephesians 4:29—"Do not let any unwholesome talk come out of your mouths, but only what is helpful for building others up according to their needs, that it may benefit those who listen." This reinforces Jesus' command in the Unit Verse.

✓ Living the Lesson (5-10 minutes)

Work out a "telephone devotional" using either the Unit Verse or Ephesians 4:29, suggestions from the grape cluster on supporting friends and a sentence closing prayer. Let kids take turns participating and record the devotional. You might even choose to have everyone sing a verse of "Jesus Loves Me."

Close class by having kids each tell the person on their left one thing they like about him/her.

> **Optional:** If desired give each student a purple happy face sticker to remind them to be "grape" kids and avoid using put-downs.

Words of Friendship

You're the GREATEST!

I'm Sorry

I LIKE YOU! CAN WE GET TO KNOW EACH OTHER?

I'm Glad You're My Friend! Because:

Unsolved Mysteries

In each case below, a crime of "verbicide" has been committed. Read the situation and decide what the crime is, who is the criminal, and what the results are.

Bob and Mike have been best friends for a long time. Bob has a learning disability that makes it difficult for him to read. Today Mike got mad at Bob. "You're just a dummy!" he shouted angrily.

_____

_____

_____

_____

_____

Kevin stopped over at Todd's house after school. He saw a boom box on the table and wanted to listen to it. The boom box belongs to Owen, Todd's older brother. "I'll have to ask Owen first," Todd said. Then Kevin shot back, "You're just a chicken."

_____

_____

_____

_____

_____

Bonnie and Ellen have been friends since first grade. Ellen has been wanting to become friends with Amber and Heather because they are part of the "in" crowd at school. Amber asked, "What became of you and Bonnie? I thought you were such good friends?" "Yea," added Heather. "She's such a goody-goody always going to church and reading her Bible." Ellen answered, "I know. She talks about Jesus so much I can't stand it any-more." Suddenly Ellen saw Bonnie standing near-by and knew she had heard the conversation.

_____

_____

_____

_____

_____

Lesson 4

Will You Still Be My Friend?

Aim: That your students will understand that no matter what changes they experience in their friendships they can have Jesus as their unchanging, forever friend.

Scripture: John 15:12-17

Unit Verse: My command is this: Love each other as I have loved you. John 15:12

Unit Affirmation: I CAN BE A FRIEND TO OTHERS AS JESUS IS A FRIEND TO ME!

 Planning Ahead

1. Photocopy activity sheet (page 111)—one for each student.
2. Photocopy activity sheet (page 112)—one for every two students. Cut out and assemble these before class.

 1 Setting the Stage (5-10 minutes)

WHAT YOU'LL DO

- Write "Friendship Acrostics" as a way to review the characteristics of good friendships

WHAT YOU'LL NEED

- Paper and pencils for the acrostics

2 Introducing the Issue (20 minutes)

WHAT YOU'LL DO

- Work in small groups to write a skit about the ways friendships change
- Discuss things that cause friendships to change and the feelings that surround the changes
- Use an activity sheet to identify the feelings that can occur when friendships change, and an important message to remember during those times
- Add a phrase to the Unit Affirmation Poster

WHAT YOU'LL NEED

- "When Friendships Change . . ." Activity Sheet (page 111)
- Unit Affirmation poster

3 Searching the Scriptures (20 minutes)

WHAT YOU'LL DO

- Recognize Jesus as the never-changing, forever friend
- Play a game to find ways to handle changes in friendships
- Write a personal creed

WHAT YOU'LL NEED

- Bibles
- "Friendship Blockbuster" Activity Sheet (page 112)

4 Living the Lesson (5-10 minutes)

WHAT YOU'LL DO

- Create a "telephone devotional" message about Jesus' desire to be everyone's forever friend
- Provide an opportunity to accept Jesus as their forever friend

WHAT YOU'LL NEED

- Bibles
- Tape recorder
- "My Forever Friend" bookmark Activity Sheet (page 112)

Setting the Stage (5-10 minutes)

Before class today, put paper and pencils on the tables and write the following on the board:

A FRIEND IS . . .

A FRIEND IS NOT . . .

As students arrive, begin by reviewing some of the characteristics of a good friend. **What are some of the qualities you value in a friend?** Allow the kids to answer and then instruct them to write (individually or in pairs) "Friendship Acrostics" by copying what is on the board onto their papers, and writing the word "FRIEND" vertically down the left-hand side of their paper. Then have them add a word or phrase that fits the heading and begins with each of the letters down the side. Example: A Friend is . . . F–Forgiving, R–Ready to help, I–Interesting to talk to; E–Encouraging; N–Nice to me; D–Devoted. Encourage them to be creative and think carefully about the characteristics they want to list.

When all are completed, ask each one (or pair) to read their acrostic to the class. Then, as a group, decide on the best word or phrase for each letter, and write those on the board.

Introducing the Issue (20 minutes)

Wouldn't it be nice if all our friends were like the first acrostic, all the time? And wouldn't it be nice if nothing ever happened to change those special friendships? Unfortunately, that's not the way things work. You can know *for sure* that sometimes your friends will let you down, and that things will happen to change your relationships with friends you care about.

Divide the class into groups of two or three and instruct them to think of several things that could happen to change friendships. Tell them to be very specific. As they are working, circulate among the groups and listen to their responses. After a few minutes, help each group focus on one of their choices, being sure that there is no duplication between groups and that none of the groups knows what the others have chosen.

When each group has one, give them five minutes to work out a short skit depicting their situation. After the time is up, let each group present their skit for the rest of the class. When all the skits have been presented, ask the kids to briefly share some of the other reasons, they thought of earlier, that friendships change. Possible reasons might include: Moving away; New friends seem more interesting than old friends; Interests change (someone joins the swim team); Betrayal of trust (telling secrets); Starting a new school (middle school or Jr. High); Get mad and stay mad (rather than work it out); Death (extreme, but it happens!); Revenge (you hurt me so I'm going to hurt you back).

Distribute copies of the activity sheet "When Friendships Change . . ." (page 111). **Although it is a fact of life that friendships change, none of us likes it when it happens. Changes of all kinds can churn up all kinds of feelings inside us** As an example of this, ask the kids to put their arms on top of the table and fold their hands, noticing which thumb is on top. Then tell them to unfold their hands, and refold them, being sure the *other* thumb is on top this time. As small a change as this is, it feels uncomfortable. Help kids see that a change in friendships is a much *bigger* change, and therefore causes much bigger feelings.

Look at the activity sheet and read the opening sentence together. Work together as a group to identify feelings that can be drawn on the faces. Be sure to validate each feeling as it is shared. It is OK to feel a wide range of feelings when friendships change! People around them may try to talk them out of their feelings. But almost *everyone* feels the same feelings, and it is important for them to know they are OK for feeling them!

Some examples of feelings include: <u>Denial</u> – (Won't believe it really happened); <u>Anger</u> – (Sometimes we are angry about something a friend did, and sometimes we are just angry that circumstances took our friend away); <u>Sad or depressed</u> – (A very normal reaction to loss of any kind); <u>Surprise </u>– (We can be caught off guard); <u>Betrayal</u> – ("How could you do this to me; I trusted you!"); <u>Abandonment</u> – ("You left me alone"); <u>Revengeful</u> – ("I'll show you; I'll get even!"); <u>Relief</u> – (Sometimes a change in a friendship is for the better; we don't always know how to get out of bad friendships and can feel relieved when we finally do).

Now look at the middle of the activity sheet, and let the kids work the puzzle. When they are complete, read the message together. (When friendships change, it's not the end. Remember to keep on trusting, and make a new friend!) Ask the kids to share what they think it means. **When friendships change and we experience all the difficult feelings we talked about today, we can face a very serious danger. That danger is that we will become so afraid of being hurt again in the future that we stop wanting to have friends. We can stop trusting people when we are afraid of getting hurt. That's why it is really important to remember that *everyone* experiences changes in their friendships, and even though it may hurt for a time, we need to keep trusting and reaching out to new friends. Otherwise, we will find ourselves alone. It's true that if we stop**

trusting others we won't get hurt again, but that's a terribly lonely way to live. Read the message from the activity sheet again.

Refer to the Unit Affirmation Poster and read aloud together the Unit Affirmation. Review each of the phrases you have already added, asking kids to review their meaning. Then, ask for ideas about what phrases could be added today. **How can I be a friend like Jesus when my friendships change?** Ideas might include: Don't try to get even; Try to work out conflicts; Accept the change and keep going; Pray and ask God for help; etc. Choose one phrase to add to the poster today.

We have been talking about what happens when our friendships change. Now let's talk about one friendship we can have that will *never* change.

Searching the Scriptures (20 minutes)

Today's Bible study contains some fundamental statements Jesus made about friendship. It reveals what true friendship is as Jesus prophesies His own death for us. The guidelines for measuring friendship are provided as well as a conditional promise for answered prayer from God the Father. While the standard for friendship is high—"Love each other as I have loved you," the power for fulfilling it is also provided—"I have called you friends . . . I chose you."

Many things can change friendships. In all of these changes we need to know that Jesus never changes and He wants to be our friend. He alone can offer the security and stability we need and desire. You will be providing an opportunity for your students to choose Jesus as their Forever Friend later in this lesson.

Read John 15:12-17 aloud to your class. Have students follow along in their Bibles. Help them to focus on Jesus' qualifications as the perfect friend by involving them in the Scripture reading. **Stop my reading when you hear something Jesus has done for us. I'll give you a hint. There are five things mentioned in these verses.** The items mentioned are: He died for His friends (vs. 13); Made known to us everything He heard from His heavenly Father (vs. 15); Chose us; Gave us the work of producing lasting fruit; Made it possible for us to receive answers when we pray to God (vs. 16).

What does Jesus' death for His friends tell us about His feelings towards people? (He loves them very much; puts their welfare above His own.) **How can we show that same kind of love toward our friends?** (By encouraging, listening and helping them; giving them our love.)

How does it make you feel to know Jesus chose you to be His friend?

(Happy; unworthy; surprised.) Knowing s/he was always last to be chosen for a game, team, or purposely left out of activities can haunt a child all the way into adulthood. Jesus chose us as His friends even though we may not have chosen to respond to that friendship. Knowing that He gladly, willingly, purposely chose each of us to be His friend is a great comfort and joy! If Jesus had not made that first choice, we would not be able to enjoy a loving relationship with Him and our heavenly Father.

What does the fact that He made known to us everything He heard from His heavenly Father tell us about Him? (He trusts us enough to confide in us.) Being able to share "secrets" is a special part of friendship. Jesus has opened Himself up to us and let us in on the "family secrets."

Jesus says that He gave us the job of bearing fruit. That means bringing others to join His family and enjoy His friendship. Knowing that Jesus has given us something to do that is really lasting and meaningful lets us know how important we are. **What has He promised us when we carry out the job of bearing fruit?** (That God the Father will give us whatever we ask in Jesus' name.) **Why should we do what Jesus commands?** (Because we love Him.) Point out that because He is Lord and God, Jesus could simply demand that we obey Him without question. However, Jesus bases our obedience on our love for Him. When we experience His wonderful love and care we will be excited and happy to tell others about our best Friend.

Many churches use a creed to express their faith in God. A creed is simply a brief series of sentences that begin with the words "I believe . . ." that tell what we believe about God or Jesus. Pass out sheets of paper and have your students write a personal creed on Jesus' friendship based on John 15:12-17. An example might be: I believe Jesus chose me to be His friend. I believe He died to show me how much He loves me. I believe . . . I believe . . . I believe . . . Have kids write five of these statements. They can take these home and hang them up in their rooms.

Be aware of students who may not have made a decision to follow Jesus. If they are uncomfortable with this activity let them write a creed a Bible character might have written. Suggested characters are: Peter; Zacchaeus; Paul; Martha.

To help find ways to handle changes in their friendships, your students will play a game with the Friendship Blockbuster from page 112. Divide your class into pairs. In each pair the kids will take turns throwing the block and brainstorming ways to handle the situation thrown. Allow several minutes for playing this game then share ideas. Friends are vital to preteens and a change in a friendship can be as devastating as a death. Because they may have experienced bad breakups they may express feelings parallel to steps in

grieving: shock; denial; anger; guilt; depression; acceptance; and/or renewal. Keep the focus on positive ways to handle the changes presented in the game. Guide your kids into not only dealing with their own feelings but to reach out to their friends as well. When they know that Jesus will never change in His unconditional love for them, they are set free to extend that love to others. Not all friendships will be restored, but Jesus gives the power to go on and make new, stronger friendships.

The Unit Verse for this unit is found in the Bible basis for today's lesson. **Let's discover how Jesus handled changes in His friendships.** Have kids look up the following verses: John 11:33-36 (was sad and cried); 21:12, 13 (went out of His way to spend time with them); Luke 22: 60-62 and John 21:15-17 (gave them another chance). These are good examples for us to remember. Because Jesus understands what it's like, He can help us through changes in our friendships, too.

☑ Living the Lesson (5-10 minutes)

Use the Unit Verse, some ideas from its discussion or suggestions from the game, and a sentence prayer to create a "telephone devotional." Be sure every student has an opportunity sometime in this unit study to have a part in the devotional. Record the message.

Hand out the bookmarks and let students cut them out. **Jesus tells us He has already chosen us to be His friends. He is willing and able to be an unchanging, loving friend to each of you. Now you have an opportunity to choose Him for your Forever Friend. If you have already asked Jesus to be your Forever Friend or choose to do so now, write your name in the blank on this bookmark.** Lead in prayer, allowing students to also pray silently and talk to Jesus. Close class by singing the first verse of "What a Friend We Have in Jesus."

When Friends Change...

When things happen to change our friendships, we all experience similar feelings. Write the names of some of those feelings under each of the circles. Then, draw a face in the circle that shows that feeling.

SECRET MESSAGE: Break the following code to discover an important message about friendships.

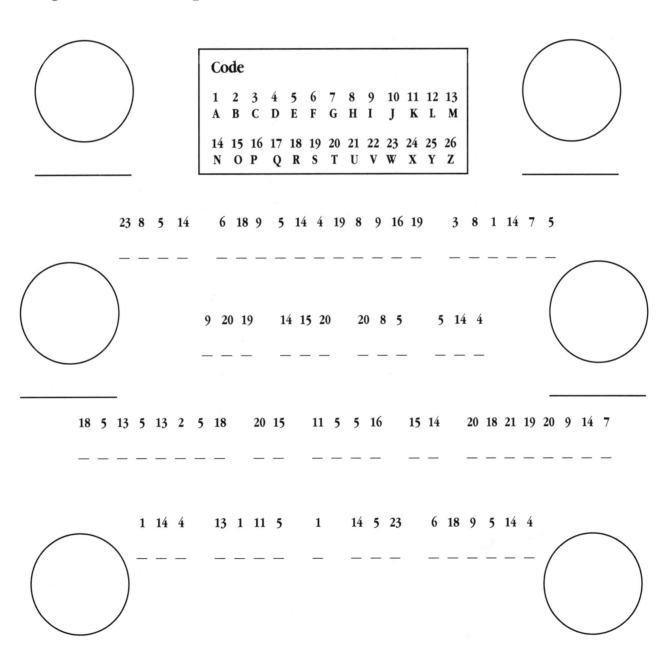

Code

1	2	3	4	5	6	7	8	9	10	11	12	13
A	B	C	D	E	F	G	H	I	J	K	L	M

14	15	16	17	18	19	20	21	22	23	24	25	26
N	O	P	Q	R	S	T	U	V	W	X	Y	Z

23 8 5 14   6 18 9 5 14 4 19 8 9 16 19   3 8 1 14 7 5

_ _ _ _   _ _ _ _ _ _ _ _ _ _   _ _ _ _ _ _

9 20 19   14 15 20   20 8 5   5 14 4

_ _ _   _ _ _   _ _ _   _ _ _

18 5 13 5 13 2 5 18   20 15   11 5 5 16   15 14   20 18 21 19 20 9 14 7

_ _ _ _ _ _ _ _   _ _   _ _ _ _   _ _   _ _ _ _ _ _ _ _

1 14 4   13 1 11 5   1   14 5 23   6 18 9 5 14 4

_ _ _   _ _ _ _   _   _ _ _   _ _ _ _ _ _

Cut on solid lines only; Fold on dotted lines; form a block and glue together so that printing is on the outside.

#3

Fold in and glue to back of #1

Kelly has to move to another state.

Fold in and glue to back of #2

Fold in and glue to back of #3 (#4)

Jon says if you don't do things his way he won't be your friend Anymore.

Ann and you began classes in a bigger school, now she ignores you.

Jason made the ball team but you didn't. You don't see much of each other now.

fold in and glue to #4

#1

Erin's parents got divorced. Now she avoids you.

#2

You accepted Jesus as your savior. Scott calls you "goody-goody" and won't be your friend anymore.

Bookmark—make one for each sdtudent

I have called you friends. John 15:15

(name)

Jesus Is My Forever Friend

Can You Keep a Secret?

Aim: That your students will understand that God wants us to be trustworthy and not betray a friend's confidence.

Scripture: 1 Samuel 20:5-42

Unit Verse: My command is this: Love each other as I have loved you. John 15:12

Unit Affirmation: I CAN BE A FRIEND TO OTHERS AS JESUS IS A FRIEND TO ME!

 Planning Ahead

1. Photocopy activity sheets (pages 119 and 120)—one for each student.
2. Write questions on the board for SETTING THE STAGE.
3. Make two 9" x 12" signs. One says "Agree" and the other "Disagree."
4. Read I Samuel 20:5-42 through several times.

1 Setting the Stage (5-10 minutes)

WHAT YOU'LL DO

- Play "Reporter" to introduce the subject of secrets and confidentiality

WHAT YOU'LL NEED

- Paper and pencils

2 Introducing the Issue (20 minutes)

WHAT YOU'LL DO

- Participate in an Agree/Disagree exercise to generate discussion about keeping or not keeping secrets
- Add a phrase to the Unit Affirmation Poster and review what it tells us about being a good friend

WHAT YOU'LL NEED

- "To Tell or Not to Tell . . . " Activity Sheet (page 119)
- "Agree" and "Disagree" signs
- Unit Affirmation Poster

3 Searching the Scriptures (20 minutes)

WHAT YOU'LL DO

- Identify problems arising from loss of confidentiality
- Pantomime scenes of a story to discover how Jonathan's trustworthiness saved David's life.
- Write answers in a newspaper advice column to consider ways to keep their friends' trust.

WHAT YOU'LL NEED

- Bibles
- "Dear Gabby" Activity Sheet (page 120)

4 Living the Lesson (5-10 minutes)

WHAT YOU'LL DO

- Add to the "telephone devotional"
- Write out a prayer about friendship and trust

WHAT YOU'LL NEED

- Bibles
- Tape recorder
- Markers

☑ Setting the Stage (5-10 minutes)

As kids enter the room, give them pieces of paper and pencils. Tell them that for the next few minutes, they are going to be reporters, trying to get some interesting information from the other members of the class. To play, let them spend time talking to each other about the questions on the board. When they are the listener, they are to take notes, so they can "report" later on. They can talk with as many kids as possible until you call "time."

Questions on the board:

1. What was the best trip or vacation you've ever taken? (If they have never been on a trip or vacation, where would they most like to go on one?)

2. What is your favorite TV show? Your least favorite TV show?

3. Name one person you REALLY admire and want to be like someday, and why.

4. What is your deepest secret? Maybe something you've never told anyone before?

NOTE: You will need to be sensitive to this last question, in that it could raise some anxiety in your kids who do have painful issues they have never discussed with anyone. You can handle this in two ways: As they begin, tell everyone that the only rule of the game is that all have the "right to pass" and not answer any of the questions, and then be sure to circulate during the game and remind them of the rule if you see a child feeling uncomfortable.

☑ Introducing the Issue (20 minutes)

Let's see what kind of reporters we have here today. What kind of a travelogue can we write based on where everyone has been or would like to go? (Kids share responses from question one.)

Now let's write a TV review column. Talk about the best and worst TV shows. **How about a feature story about "Heroes."** Talk about the people shared as most admired.

No newspaper would be complete without a gossip column. What great secrets did you find out about your classmates? Play up the fact that most likely, no one shared their true deepest secret. Consider this part of the paper a "flop," and move on.

Today we are going to talk about telling and keeping secrets. Each of us has things that happen to us, or feelings that we feel deep inside that we don't want to tell the whole world. In our reporter game, it was safe to talk about places we've been or would like to go or what TV shows we

like or don't like. But telling our deepest secrets is *not* something we do publicly.

However, God has designed us so that we *need* to share the deepest feelings in our hearts. That is a part of life that is good, and one of the best parts about having close, trusted friends. However, sometimes it is hard to know when to tell our secrets to someone else, and it can be even *harder* to know what to do when someone tells their secrets to us!

Pass out copies of the activity sheet, "To Tell or Not to Tell" (page 119). Give students time to complete them individually.

As they are working, post "Agree" and "Disagree" signs on opposite sides of the room. When everyone has finished their activity sheets, lead a discussion of each statement. Before you talk about each one, however, ask the kids to stand under the sign that indicates how they answered the statement. Be sure to prepare them for this by emphasizing that there are no "right" or "wrong" answers; they are simply expressing their opinions.

Begin by reading the first statement, and asking the kids to move to the appropriate side of the room. When all have placed themselves, ask volunteers on each side to say why they answered as they did. Then, discuss the statement, using the information below if it hasn't already come out from the kids themselves.

When you are finished with the first statement, move on to the second, repeating the process as outlined above.

#1: We have already talked about this one. Sharing secrets is an important part of friendship.

#2: Although generally speaking, most secrets are to be kept confidential, there ARE some secrets that should NOT be kept. The general rule about this is that if we know a friend is either hurting themselves, or being hurt by someone else, we need to do something about that. We can find a trusted adult to help.

#3: We can decide how much we want to tell others about ourselves. However, telling secrets about someone else can hurt them very badly, and is *not* to be done (with the exception noted in #2)

#4: Encourage kids to get help when they need it! They should always feel free to talk to a trusted adult when they need to.

#5: If you are telling someone else's secrets without their permission, it is *your* problem, and your friend has a right to be upset with you.

Finish the poster today by adding an appropriate phrase, as you have in weeks past. Then, review all the statements as a way to reinforce what it means to be a friend to others as Jesus is a friend to us. **Sometimes it can be hard to know just how to be a good friend! Let's see what two friends in**

the Bible had to go through together.

 # Searching the Scriptures (20 minutes)

Do today's story as a pantomime with small groups of kids acting out different scenes of the Bible story. Before class read I Samuel 20:5-42 over several times noting how the scenes change and where students can change parts. Have kids take turns playing David and Jonathan in different scenes. You will also need people for Saul, Abner, and the servant boy. (If your enrollment is small, students will have to participate in more than one scene.) Ask kids to turn to the Scripture passage and follow along. Read aloud slowly to allow students to pantomime the action. Pause to allow kids to take turns in new scenes after these verses: 9; 17; 24a; 25; 29; 34; 40; 42. If you have a large class and several good readers, you might want to have students also take turns reading the Bible text.

When King Saul tried to kill him, David told Jonathan where he was going to hide. What does that show us about their friendship? (David trusted Jonathan completely, even with his life.) **The real characteristic of a good friendship is being able to share secrets and trust each other.**

Have you ever blown into a fuzzy, white dandelion? What happens? (Seeds are sent every direction; the flower is ruined.) **Can you gather the seeds up and restore the flower?** (No.) **That's similar to what happens when a person betrays a friend's trust. Once a secret is told, trust is broken and it is difficult, sometimes impossible, to restore it.**

What did Jonathan promise to do for David? (Find out if his father really wanted to kill him and let him know; protect him and send him away safely.) **What did Jonathan ask David to promise him?** (Always be kind to him and his family.) **Both of these friends really trusted and cared for each other. What do you think would have happened if Jonathan had told his father where David was?** (Saul would have gone out, caught David, and killed him.)

How do you think Jonathan felt about being caught between loyalty to his friend, David, and loyalty to his father, King Saul? (Upset; confused; unhappy.) **Sometimes friendships can be costly. What did Jonathan's promise to help David cost him?** Look in verses 41, 42. (Sadness; separation from his friend.) **Jonathan could have joined David and started a rebellion against wicked Saul, but instead he chose to obey God and remain loyal to his father. The ultimate price he paid was his death.**

Jonathan respected David's need for secrecy and told no one of the plan which would save David's life. Confidentiality or keeping a secret is very important. However, are there times you might need to tell some-

one else something your friend told you? When? Although the emphasis in this lesson is on keeping a friend's confidence, present-day society has forced on us some circumstances in which we need to share that secrecy with others. Child abuse, alcohol, and other drug misuse or any action which endangers the life of the friend require us to walk a fine line between breaking a confidence and helping a friend.

Optional: Have someone look up Proverbs 11:13—"A gossip betrays a confidence, but a trustworthy man keeps a secret." **What is gossip?** (Repeating what one knows or hears about other people and their business.)

If you have time, let your students experience this firsthand by playing the game "Gossip." Have everyone form a circle. Whisper this sentence to one person in the circle: "God wants us to be trustworthy and not betray a friend's confidence." Have each student whisper the sentence once to the kid on their left. The last person to receive it repeats it out loud. Then repeat the original sentence. It probably changed considerably as it was passed along. When we gossip, the truth gets all mixed up.

Sometimes we feel like Jonathan caught between his father and his friend when our friends tell us something that we know is a danger to them and where they need help. How do you decide when you should keep a friend's secret and when you should tell it to someone else? The thing we need to keep in mind is that we are to love each other as Jesus loves us. That means trying to protect and help our friends first of all.

Pass out copies of "Dear Gabby" activity sheet (page 120). Students will pretend they are writing an advice column and answer problems sent in to a newspaper. This gives them an opportunity to find ways to keep their friends' trust. Let kids work on this page individually then discuss answers together.

Did "Mighty Mouth" help or harm her friend Kim? Explain your answer. (Harm. She was really gossiping and betraying Kim's trust.) **What do you think "Mighty" could do to straighten out this mess?** (She could apologize to Kim; try not to tell things about her again.) **What do you think might happen as a result of this girl's betrayal of her friend's confidence?** (Kim might never give her another chance; no one else would trust her again.)

What do you think "Wondering" should do about Steve? Answers may differ. He could tell a school counselor, nurse, or Steve's parents about his drinking problem. Although this kind of telling might be helpful to Steve it would also probably alienate him. Perhaps a wise thing to do would be to talk to Steve about it first. You could tell him that you think he needs help with his problem. Give him a period of time, say a week, to tell someone himself. If he

hasn't done so in that length of time, inform him that you intend to tell a trusted adult about it.

The situation with "Concerned" is similar to that of Steve which was discussed previously, but brings out the opportunity for a Sunday school teacher or pastor to visit the home and intervene for Keshia. Both situations highlight the need for prayer before action.

✓ Living the Lesson (5-10 minutes)

Complete your "telephone devotional" series by using the Unit Verse, a few suggestions on how to keep a friend's confidence and a sentence prayer. Tape it.

Close by having students write out individual prayers about friendship and trust in color. They might express happiness with yellow; anger with red; sadness with blue; confusion or fear with gray; jealousy or envy with green; a desire to improve with a rainbow of colors. Remind them that no matter what their previous experience has been with friends, Jesus will always be their best Friend and they can tell Him all their secrets. He loves them and will understand and help them.

To Tell, or Not to Tell...

This is an Agree/Disagree activity. Read each statement carefully, and place an X on the line that tells whether you AGREE or DISAGREE with it.

Agree Disagree

_____ _____ **1.** It's best NOT to tell my secrets to anyone; my private stuff is none of their business anyway.

_____ _____ **2.** It's always wrong to tell somebody else the secrets a friend tells to me.

_____ _____ **3.** Telling secrets about myself is OK; telling secrets about someone else is NOT OK.

_____ _____ **4.** Sometimes telling secrets to an adult is better than telling my secrets to someone my own age.

_____ _____ **5.** If my friend gets mad at me for telling one little person something they told me, that's his/her problem!

DEAR GABBY

Dear Gabby, Kim told me she liked Jeff. I promised not to tell anyone. Then today I saw Brenda had a heart on the inside of her notebook with Jeff + Brenda written on it. I asked her if Jeff really liked her. Brenda said "Yes." Then I blurted out that was too bad because Kim liked him. Now Brenda is telling everyone Kim has a crush on Jeff. Kim is mad at me and I feel terrible. What should I do? Mighty Mouth

Dear Mighty,

_____

_____

_____

_____

_____

_____

Dear Gabby, My friend Steve has a locker next to mine. The other day I saw him take out a paper bag. There was a liquor bottle inside the bag and Steve took a drink from it. Then he slipped it back inside the locker. When he realized I saw him, he said, "If you're my friend, you won't tell." I don't want to lose

Steve's friendship, but I think I should tell someone about his drinking. What do you think? Wondering

Dear Wondering,

_____

_____

_____

_____

_____

_____

Dear Gabby, I'm worried about my friend, Keshia. She is in my Sunday school class and always has a lot of bruises on her arms. She says they are because she is a klutz and is always banging herself up. But last week she wasn't in class. I stopped by her house to invite her to our skating party. She had a black eye and a cut on her forehead. At first she said she ran into the door when she got up to use the bathroom the other night, but then she started to tell me something more. Her dad came home and she stopped talking. After he went in the other room, she began to cry and told me not to tell anyone about her black eye. I think her dad beats up on her. I'm worried about Keshia. How can I help her? Concerned

Dear Concerned,

_____

_____

_____

_____

_____

_____

Service Projects for Friendship

✔ 1. You can emphasize another aspect of what it means to be a friend to others as Jesus is a friend to us by getting your class involved in a project to donate food and/or clothes to a nearby food and clothing distribution center. Find out in advance from the center what kind of food they most need, and how you can prepare clothing (washed, sorted, etc.). Then, ask the kids to sign up to bring various food items which you will pack in boxes as a class. If you will be collecting clothing, ask the kids to bring their own used clothing to share with other children. Be sure to send a letter home to the parents explaining what you are doing and inviting their cooperation. On the last week of the unit, arrange a time for the class to deliver these items to the center together.

✔ 2. One of the best things we can do for our friends who are not Christians is to share with them what it means to have Jesus as our friend. Plan an outreach party for your kids to invite their friends who do not attend church. Perhaps an unbirthday theme would be appropriate. Conduct it as an old–fashioned birthday party with lots of party games and food, and a rousing chorus of "Happy Unbirthday to Us!" Then, end the time with a short devotional explaining how kids can have a second birthday to celebrate becoming a member of God's family. Explain what that means and the security that comes from being a child of God and having Jesus as our friend.

✔ 3. Your class can use the skits in this section to present a program for a younger class, nursing home, homeless shelter, Bible camp, VBS, or day camp. The skits could be adapted for puppet use and be presented that way instead of with kid actors.

✔ 4. You might like to videotape the week-by-week devotional with several kids reading the Scripture and tips. Since this same Unit Verse activity is used throughout the unit, kids could take turns from week to week. This would allow each student to participate. The videos could be shown at a club parent night, church or Sunday school program or party.

✔ 5. Make a friendship fruit or vegetable salad or soup by having each kid bring one item. As you mix all the ingredients together, talk about friendship. Just as the salad or soup wouldn't taste as good if one part was missing, so it is with each one of them. When one of them is left out an essential ingredient of your relationships is missing. When all the kids are added together they make the class, group, or friendships terrific!